D0671739

Concerning the four bonus pages in the comic book…
"I can't believe you revealed the heroine's measurements. I'm disappointed." "Well done, Watsuki! Good job!" It's interesting to hear opinions that are the complete opposite. The bonus pages are my way of thanking the people who bought the manga. They sometimes contain spoilers, so after you've read the manga, please check them out when you have the time.

—Nobuhiro Watsuki

Nobuhiro Watsuki earned international accolades for his first major manga series, **Rurouni Kenshin**, about a wandering swordsman in Meiji Era Japan. Serialized in Japan's *Weekly Shonen Jump* from 1994 to 1999, **Rurouni Kenshin**, available in North America from VIZ Media, quickly became a worldwide sensation, inspiring a spin-off short story ("Yahiko no Sakabatô"), an animated TV show and a series of novels. Watsuki's latest hit, **Buso Renkin**, began publication in *Weekly Shonen Jump* in June 2003.

BUSO RENKIN
VOL. 2
The SHONEN JUMP ADVANCED
Manga Edition

STORY AND ART BY
NOBUHIRO WATSUKI

Translation and English Adaptation/Mayumi Kobayashi
Touch-up Art & Lettering/James Gaubatz
Design/Yukiko Whitley
Editor/Urian Brown

Managing Editor/Frances E. Wall
Editorial Director/Elizabeth Kawasaki
VP & Editor in Chief/Yumi Hoashi
Sr. Director of Acquisitions/Rika Inouye
Sr. VP of Marketing/Liza Coppola
Exec. VP of Sales & Marketing/John Easum
Publisher/Hyoe Narita

BUSOU RENKIN © 2003 by Nobuhiro Watsuki. All rights reserved.
First published in Japan in 2003 by SHUEISHA Inc., Tokyo.
English translation rights in the United States of America and Canada arranged by SHUEISHA Inc. The stories, characters and incidents mentioned in this publication are entirely fictional.

No portion of this book may be reproduced or transmitted in any form or by any means without written permission from the copyright holders.

Printed in the U.S.A.

Published by VIZ Media, LLC
P.O. Box 77010
San Francisco, CA 94107

SHONEN JUMP ADVANCED Manga Edition
10 9 8 7 6 5 4 3 2 1
First printing, October 2006

www.viz.com

PARENTAL ADVISORY
BUSO RENKIN is rated T+ for Older Teen and is recommended for ages 16 and up. This volume contains fantasy violence.

Vol. 2
Fade to Black

STORY & ART BY
NOBUHIRO WATSUKI

Alchemy: An early scientific practice that that swept through all of Europe, and combines elements of various disciplines. Such studies were based on the transmutation of base metals into gold, and the preparation of the Elixir of Immortality, none of which succeeded. However, unknown to the public, two alchemic studies achieved success of super-paranormal proportions—the Homunculus and Kakugane.

Kazuki Muto

He was killed by a Homunculus but came back to life after Tokiko, an Alchemist Warrior, gave him the "Kakugane" as a replacement heart. He's 16 years old—a year older than his sister, Mahiro. Kazuki's Buso Renkin is a lance. (He is currently working hard to think up a cool name for it.)

CHARACTERS

Kakugane: A super-paranormal alloy that uses the most advanced alchemic technology. It is activated by one's survival instincts, the deepest part of the human psyche. It can heighten one's ability to heal, and can also become a one-of-a-kind weapon by materializing the wielder's fighting instincts. The weapon is called the Buso Renkin; each differs in shape and function.

Tokiko Tsumura

One of the Alchemist Warriors who are selectively chosen amongst those who know alchemy and are considered to be a Buso Renkin expert. Tokiko's Buso Renkin is a Death Scythe called the Valkyrie Skirt.

Kouji Rokumasu

Hideyuki Okakura

Masashi Daihama

Mahiro Muto

STORY

Alchemist Warrior Tokiko used herself as bait to lure out a man-eating Homunculus when Kazuki Muto, an unsuspecting high school student, tried to save her—and was killed. But Kazuki received a new lease on life when Tokiko gave him the "Kakugane," which was activated by his fighting instincts, and formed a new Buso Renkin, which he used to vanquish the Homunculus! Thus, a new Homunculus-busting team was formed...

A new threat emerges when Papillon Mask, the Creator of the Homunculus, attacks Tokiko with a Homunculus core that turns humans into Homunculi. Although Tokiko manages to prevent the core from entering her brain, it lodges itself within her stomach. The only way she can be saved is to capture the Creator, who can make an antidote, within a week. After discovering that the Creator is a third-year student at Kazuki's Ginsei Academy, the hunt is on! On the fourth day of their search, Kazuki is challenged by a Homunculus named Kawazui, and agrees to a one-on-one battle in order to protect a weakened Tokiko. During the battle, Kazuki realizes a new power of his Buso Renkin—the cloth on the end of it turns into energy when it resonates with his will to fight. Cornering Kawazui, Kazuki tries to find out where the Creator is, but just before getting the information, collapses from exhaustion. He awakens to find a concerned Tokiko by his side ...

The Papillon Mask Creator

Homunculus

An artificial life form created though alchemic research. Once the Homunculus core created from an organism's cell lodges itself in the human brain, it will take control of the host's body. The core alters the compounds of the body, which takes on physical attributes of the original organism. A Homunculus can only be destroyed by the power of alchemy.

Homunculus Washio

BUSO RENKIN
Volume 2: Fade to Black

CONTENTS

Chapter 8: Lock On	7
Chapter 9: The Other New Life	27
Chapter 10: VS. Washio: Section 1	47
Chapter 11: VS. Washio: Part 2: Section 1	67
Chapter 12: VS. Washio: Part 2: Section 2	87
Chapter 13: VS. Washio: Part 3	107
Chapter 14: Midnight Run 2	127
Chapter 15: Dark, Hot and Sweet	145
Chapter 16: Butterfly of Black Death	165
Chapter 17: Fade to Black	185

CHAPTER 8: LOCK-ON

WHOAAA?!
BA BAM
AAAAH?
HOTEL GINSEIKAN
BAM
UWAAAH.
YOU'RE FINALLY AWAKE.
WHAT HAPPENED TO ME?
HOTEL + ONLY IN UNDERWEAR + TOKIKO IN NORMAL CLOTHES!
HAA
HAA

READ THIS WAY
NO-THING.
ABSOLUTELY ...
WHAT WERE YOU THINKING?
YOU FELL ASLEEP AFTER THE BATTLE LAST NIGHT SO I BROUGHT YOU TO A HOTEL. IT WAS CLOSER THAN THE DORM.
DID YOU THINK I LIVED ON A CLOUD, EATING MIST?
CHUCKLE
I LIVE HERE TEMPORARILY WHILE I STAY IN THIS CITY.
I SEE.
I'M JUST SURPRISED.
IS THIS A BUSINESS HOTEL?
WHOAAA.
YOU'RE SO RUDE!
...
WHY ARE YOU ASKING SUDDENLY?
HEY, WHICH SCHOOL DO YOU GO TO AND WHAT YEAR ARE YOU?
I DON'T KNOW ANYTHING ABOUT TOKIKO.
COME TO THINK OF IT...

I DON'T GO TO SCHOOL.
HUH?
THAT UNIFORM IS FROM THE SCHOOL WHERE I WAS OPERATING UNDERCOVER BEFORE I CAME HERE.
I DIDN'T RETURN TO THE MAIN SQUAD AND CAME STRAIGHT HERE SO THAT'S WHY I'M STILL USING IT.
THE MAIN SQUAD?
...IT'S A GROUP THAT COMBATS THOSE WHO USE ALCHEMY FOR EVIL.
THAT'S ALL I CAN TELL YOU.
IF I WENT TO SCHOOL...
I WOULD BE A THIRD-YEAR IN HIGH SCHOOL.
OH! SO YOU ARE OLDER THAN ME!
DOES IT MAKE YOU HAPPY THAT I'M OLDER?
?
BUT ...
WHY DID YOU DROP OUT OF SCHOOL AND...
BECOME A WARRIOR?

READ THIS WAY
AH
CHILL
TODAY'S SATURDAY SO WE'LL BE OUT ON THE FIELD ALL DAY.
NEVER MIND ME, THE CREATOR IS OUR PRIORITY.
OH, OKAY.
FWIP
GUZZLE
SORRY ...
...I GUESS IT WAS A TOUCHY SUBJECT.
LET'S GO!
OKAY!
TOKIKO FIGHTS AGAINST MAN-EATING MONSTERS TO PROTECT EVERYONE.
CLAK
THAT'S ALL I NEED TO KNOW NOW!
BECAUSE I HATE ALL...
HOMUNCULI.

DAY 5

THE ONLY OTHER BUILDING THAT STUDENTS USE OTHER THAN THE SCHOOL IS...

"THINK ABOUT IT. THE SCHOOL ISN'T THE ONLY BUILDING STUDENTS USE ON CAMPUS."

THE ENEMY YOU DESTROYED SAID...

I CAN'T THINK OF ANYONE.
NO ONE IN MY CLASS.
SOMEONE OUT FOUR DAYS IN A ROW?
...I'VE BEEN WONDERING... THERE AREN'T A LOT OF PEOPLE AROUND TODAY.
OH, THAT'S BECAUSE IT'S SATURDAY. MORE THAN HALF THE RESIDENTS GO HOME FOR THE WEEKEND.
HUH?
TO BE HONEST, IT'S A BIT HARD TO GET AN IDEA OF HIS FEATURES WITH THE DESCRIPTION SHEET WE'VE BEEN USING.
WHAT?
OH BUT ...
Arm band Green. Height 175-180cm.
Skinny. Good posture.
Black hair, split in the front.
Long face. Pointy chin.
Pointy nose. Has a large mouth.
The edge of his eyes go up.
Thin, high eyebrows.
Pale but more of a sickly pale.
High-pitched voice.
I'M GOING TO SNEAK INTO THE SCHOOL AND CHECK THE ATTENDANCE SHEETS.
I GOT IT. YOU KEEP SEARCHING THE DORM.
SURE THING.
I SEE. THEN I DOUBT TALKING TO PEOPLE IS GOING TO GIVE US MANY LEADS.

I'M A MASTER AT DRAWING PEOPLE'S FACES!!
DON'T WORRY! NO POINT IN HIDING IT...
FLASH
...YOU'RE TALKING WITHOUT THINKING RIGHT NOW AREN'T YOU?
CLAP
I SEE. SHOULD WE DRAW A SKETCH?
THAT'S IT!
BUT I CAN'T DRAW WELL.
...
...
HE HAS BLACK HAIR AND IT'S SEPARATED IN FRONT.
LET'S START WITH HIS HAIRSTYLE.
JEEZ ...
IT'S OKAY! IT'S OKAY!
HERE.
BUT IT DOESN'T LOOK LIKE HIM!
HE'S GOOD!
DONE!

DA DUM

AAH! IT'S A WEIRDO!

NEVER MIND THAT. WHO IS TOKIKO REALLY?

...BY THE WAY, WHERE DID YOU STAY LAST NIGHT?

LEAVE ME ALONE! DANG IT!

Uh-huh. Uh-huh.
PASSION
WHAT'S WRONG WITH OKAKURA?
HE'S UHH ...
MAGAZINE: NAUGHTY BEAUTIFUL WOMAN
DOES IT MAKE YOU HAPPY THAT I'M OLDER?
!!!
HMM...
LET'S SEE...
PASSION!!
OLDER!!
OLDER WHAT? BROTHER?
YEAH.
WELL, WE'RE NOT DOING ANYTHING SO LET'S HELP HIM OUT.

READ THIS WAY
HEIGHT 175-180CM.
HE'S SKINNY AND HAS GOOD POSTURE.
HE HAS BLACK HAIR THAT'S SPLIT IN THE FRONT.
HE'S PALE BUT MORE LIKE A SICKLY PALE.
THIS IS A LITTLE MORE USEFUL THAN YOUR SKETCH.
I DON'T THINK IT'LL BE TOO DIFFICULT TO FIND HIM.
IS THIS THAT BAD?
IT'S MY MASTER-PIECE. I PUT MY SOUL INTO IT.
AH! LOOK OVER THERE.
HE HAS A GREEN ARMBAND SO HE'S A THIRD-YEAR.
LET'S ASK HIM.
EXCUSE ME.

I NEED TO TAKE MY PILLS.
THERE'S SOMETHING WE WANT TO ASK YOU...
SW
OH, HOLD ON A SEC.
!

IS IT HEALTHY TO TAKE SO MANY PILLS?
YEESH... HE'S TAKING ALL OF THOSE...

MY BODY WILL GIVE OUT ON ME.
BUT IF I DON'T...
IT'S NOT OKAY.

OH YEAH.
ANYWAY, WHAT DID YOU WANT?
YEAH.
ARE YOU SICK?

WE'VE ASKED AROUND BUT NO ONE KNOWS ANYONE THAT FITS THE DESCRIPTION.
WE'RE LOOKING FOR A MALE THIRD-YEAR STUDENT WHO LIVES IN THE DORM AND TOOK OFF FROM SCHOOL THE LAST FOUR DAYS.

I SEE... SO YOU'RE ...
!!
INVIS-IBLE?
THEN HE'S PROBABLY INVISIBLE.
NO-THING.
I SEE... NO ONE, EH?
HUH?
HE'S PROBABLY SOMEONE LIKE THAT.
EVERY CLASS HAS A CLASSMATE THAT NO ONE PAYS ANY ATTENTION TO. THEY DON'T EVEN NOTICE IF HE COMES TO CLASS OR NOT.
PEOPLE CAN SEE HIM, BUT DON'T NOTICE HIM...
POOR GUY.

READ THIS WAY
SW
WE HAVE THIS DRAWING OF HIM.
OTHER THAN A FEW DISTINCT FEATURES...
DO YOU KNOW ANYTHING ELSE ABOUT HIM?
OUTRA-GEOUS!
THIS IS...
ALL MY SOUL WENT INTO DRAWING IT!
YOUR FASHION SENSE IS TOTALLY WRONG!
I THINK IT'S A PRETTY FASHIONABLE MASK.
YOU THINK?
IF HE'S FOR REAL, HE'S JUST A FREAK.
THERE'S NO WAY THERE'S A GUY LIKE THAT.
EEEEEH ?!
NO, HE'S RIGHT!
SHOUT
!

!
THIS MASK IS AMAZING. BUTTERFLIES ARE WONDERFUL!

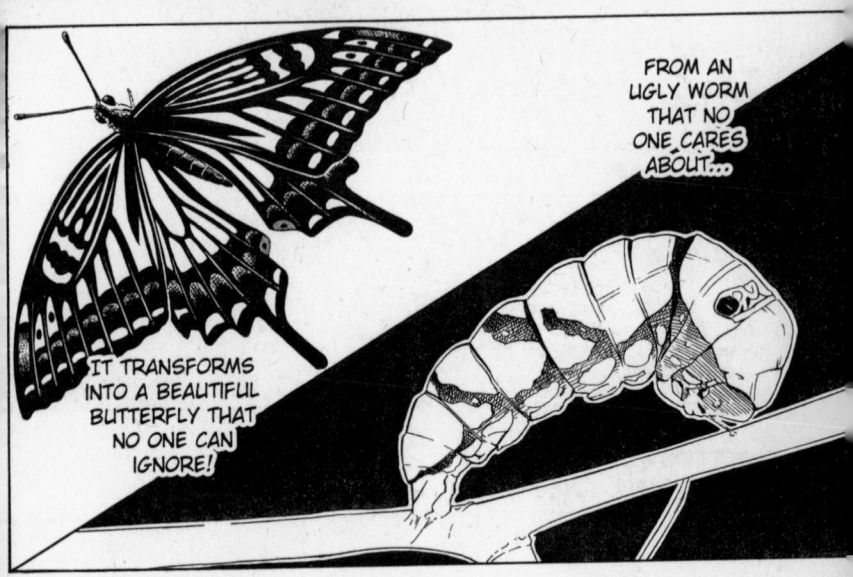
FROM AN UGLY WORM THAT NO ONE CARES ABOUT...
IT TRANSFORMS INTO A BEAUTIFUL BUTTERFLY THAT NO ONE CAN IGNORE!

HIS EYES ARE LIKE A ROTTEN SEWAGE RIVER.

YOU CAN TELL ...
BY HIS EYES.

THE PAPILLON MASK IS...
THE ELEGANT "SYMBOL OF TRANSFOR-MATION."

BLACK HAIR, SPILT IN THE FRONT.
WHAT?
MAHIRO.
HEIGHT 175~180 CM.
PALE, BUT MORE OF A SICKLY PALE...
SKINNY, GOOD POSTURE.

AH, SURE.
GET ROKUMASU AND THE OTHERS AND WAIT FOR ME AT THE ENTRANCE.
HUH? OKAY.
LET'S GET SOME LUNCH.

HE'S ALWAYS A PART OF THE BACK-GROUND.
I TOLD YOU.
HE'S INVISIBLE.
TP TP
I'VE...
LIVED HERE FOR A YEAR BUT...
I DON'T REMEMBER EVER SEEING YOU...

AND...
GACK
!!
3RD YEAR CLASSROOM C. ATTENDANCE NUMBER 8.
I FOUND HIM KAZUKI!
THERE'S DEFINITELY A THIRD-YEAR DORM RESIDENT WHO'S BEEN OUT THE LAST FOUR DAYS!
HE'S THE CREATOR, THE PAPILLON MASK!
KOUSHAKU CHOUNO, NINETEEN YEARS OLD!

BUT HE FOUND IT!
THE MAGNIFICENT POWERS OF ALCHEMY!
HFF
HFF
AND!!
HE'S A WORM THAT'S SO FRAIL HE CAN'T EVEN SUPPORT HIS OWN LIFE.
A MEANS TO MAKE AN ELEGANT TRANSFORMATION!
I HAVE TO CATCH HIM!
WOOOO
HE'S PAPILLON MASK...
IF I CATCH HIM THERE WON'T BE ANY MORE VICTIMS.
TOKIKO WILL BE SAVED!

- Height: 162 cm; Weight: 51kg
- Born: January 25th; Aquarius; Blood Type AB; 16 years old
- Favorites: Glay, math, and Weider (jelly-like drink)
- Dislikes: Nothing in particular
  (Wouldn't tell you even if I knew)
- Hobby: Computer stuff
- Things he's good at: Mimicking voices and much more
- Affiliation: Private Ginsei Academy 2nd Year High School
  Student Class Room B, Dorm resident

Character Profile No.8

Koji Rokumasu

Author's Notes

- A character created to liven up Kazuki's everyday life. He has the leveled eyebrow look (the Cool Guy) and he's in charge of the joke puns.
- The unofficial leader of the group. He usually stays in the background but he gives precise directions to resolve any issues when necessary… was my initial concept but he somehow turned out to be the man with many mysteries.
- I based Rokumasu off an anime director I went to Anime Expo with (from my comments on the cover flap of Volume 1). He held the colorful group together while he enjoyed the convention himself. I wanted to incorporate that aspect of him into a character in my story so I borrowed his likeness.

CHAPTER 9: THE OTHER NEW LIFE

THAT'S ...
STOP RIGHT THERE!
THAT'S ENOUGH.
FWEEN!

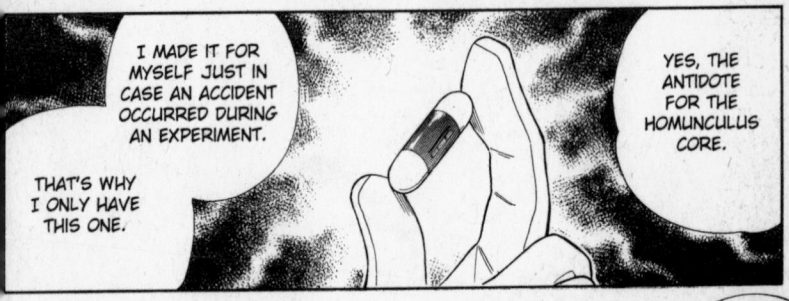
I MADE IT FOR MYSELF JUST IN CASE AN ACCIDENT OCCURRED DURING AN EXPERIMENT.
THAT'S WHY I ONLY HAVE THIS ONE.
YES, THE ANTIDOTE FOR THE HOMUNCULUS CORE.

BUT IF YOUR FRIEND DOESN'T TAKE THIS IN THE NEXT TWO DAYS SHE'LL TURN INTO A HOMUNCULUS.
I FINISHED MY FINAL EXPERIMENT SO I DON'T NEED THIS ANYMORE.

FOR YOUR KAKUGANE?
HOW ABOUT I TRADE YOU THIS...

CHAPTER 9:
THE OTHER NEW LIFE

THE OTHER ALCHEMIC CREATION, OPPOSITE OF THE HOMUNCULUS.
I'VE HEARD ABOUT IT BUT AFTER SEEING WHAT IT CAN DO, THE OTHER DAY I WANT TO STUDY IT.
WHAT ARE YOU GOING TO DO? IF YOU DON'T WANT IT I'LL LET IT GO DOWN THE DRAIN.
EVEN IF YOU WANT IT LATER, IT TAKES TIME TO MAKE IT SO IT'LL BE TOO LATE.
?
SAY
YOU
DO
WHAT
SO ...
...
CLENCH

READ THIS WAY
THAT'S WHAT I THOUGHT YOU'D SAY.
IT'S OBVIOUS YOU'LL BE AT A DISADVANTAGE IF YOU GIVE UP YOUR WEAPON.
I CAN'T!
I CAN'T GIVE YOU THIS!
JUST LIKE YOU, MY LIFE IS IMPORTANT TO ME.
YOU'RE WRONG!
?
IT'S BECAUSE IF I GIVE YOU THE KAKUGANE I'LL DIE.
THEN I WON'T BE ABLE TO DELIVER THE ANTIDOTE TO TOKIKO!
WHAT DO YOU MEAN BY THAT? TELL ME?
TOKIKO GAVE ME THE KAKUGANE TO REPLACE MY HEART AND I CAME BACK TO LIFE.
...I WAS PIERCED THROUGH THE HEART BY A HOMUNCULUS YOU CREATED AND I DIED.
THAT'S WHY THE KAKUGANE INSIDE ME ALSO ACTS AS MY NEW LIFE.

GRRR
AHHH?
YOU GOT A NEW LIFE AS EASY AS THAT?
HAA
THUMP
THUMP
THE KAKUGANE HAS THAT KIND OF POWER?
LIFE ...
NEW LIFE ...!
GIVE IT TO ME!
THIS GUY IS NUTS!
GACK
HAAAA!
GIVE ME THAT NEW LIIIIIFE!

!
CLENCH
DO YOU HAVE ANY IDEA HOW MANY PEOPLE DIED BECAUSE OF THE HOMUNCULI YOU CREATED!
YOU HAVE NO RIGHT!
WHY SHOULD YOU GET A NEW LIFE!?

!
CATCH
OH NO! I DIDN'T MEAN TO...
GFF.
AA!
?
TOKIKO!
THUD
AA
He tricked me!!
IT'S NOT SOMETHING YOU CAN GET OUT OF YOUR SYSTEM BY SWALLOWING A PILL.
THE REAL ANTIDOTE CAN ONLY BE DIRECTLY INJECTED INTO THE CORE.
NOPE. IT'S A FAKE.
IT'S THE ANTIDOTE FOR THE HOMUNCULUS CORE.
THAT'S IT!

YEAH, BUT IT'S WEIRD.
HE'S THE BOSS AND THE SOURCE OF ALL THIS BUT HE'S A WEAKLING.
BUT YOU CAUGHT THE PAPILLON MASK. GOOD JOB.

OF COURSE HE IS.
HE HASN'T BEEN TRAINED TO FIGHT LIKE ME.
HE'S A REGULAR HUMAN EXCEPT FOR THE FACT HE'S ABLE TO MANUFACTURE HOMUNCULI.

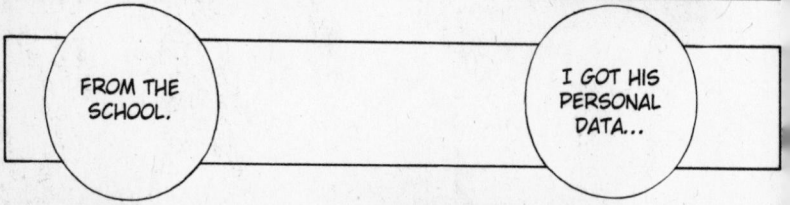
FROM THE SCHOOL.
I GOT HIS PERSONAL DATA...

HIS TOTAL ENTRANCE EXAM SCORE FROM FIVE SUBJECTS WAS FIVE HUNDRED POINTS. HIS IQ IS 230.
IF ALL WENT WELL HE WOULD HAVE BEEN THE MOST CELEBRATED GENIUS THIS SCHOOL HAS EVER SEEN.
HE'S THE FIRST-BORN SON OF A WEALTHY FAMILY WHO'S BEEN IN THE EXPORT AND IMPORT BUSINESS SINCE THE MEIJI ERA.
KOUSHAKU CHOUNO...

WITHOUT ANY TREATMENT AVAILABLE, HIS IMMUNE SYSTEM WILL FAIL AND SOON HE'LL DIE.
WOULD HAVE BEEN?
AFTER ENTERING THE SCHOOL HE DEVELOPED AN UNEXPLAINABLE ILLNESS.
EVEN THE TEACHERS HAVE GIVEN UP ON HIM.
ONLY A HANDFUL OF STUDENTS KNOW ABOUT HIM.
3-C CHOUNO
SINCE THEN HE'S LOCKED HIMSELF IN HIS ROOM.
HE'S BEEN IN AND OUT OF THE HOSPITAL AND WAS HELD BACK TWO YEARS.
DON'T YOU FEEL SORRY FOR ME?
SEE? DIDN'T I TELL YOU?
WHERE DID YOU LEARN ALCHEMY...
WHERE DID YOU FIND OUT HOW TO MANUFACTURE HOMUNCULI?
I HAVE A QUESTION.

READ THIS WAY
WHY DID YOU...
DECIDE TO CREATE MONSTERS LIKE THE HOMUNCULI?
NNN... I EVEN IMPRESS MYSELF SOMETIMES ...
GRIN
I LEARNED FROM MY GREAT-GREAT GRANDFATHER'S RESEARCH NOTES FROM HALF A CENTURY AGO. HE WAS THE ONE WHO GOT INTO THE WESTERN IMPORT AND EXPORT TRADE.
I FOUND IT IN THE STORAGE AT MY HOUSE. IT TOOK ME THREE YEARS TO COMPLETE.
AFTER I SAW THAT, MY ASSUMPTIONS WERE CONFIRMED.
I KNOW WHY.
HE'S PLANNING TO USE THIS ON HIMSELF TO BECOME A HOMUNCULUS!
THE FIRST TWENTY HOMUNCULI WERE MERE PROTOTYPES ...
IT WAS ALL TO CREATE THIS CORE. HIS TWENTY-FIRST CREATION.

HOMUNCULI CAN REGENERATE EVEN IF THEY ARE COMPLETELY SHATTERED TO BITS AS LONG AS THEY ARE DESTROYED BY NORMAL FORCE.

THEIR POWERFUL BODIES MAKE THEM THE CLOSEST THING TO BEING IMMORTAL AS ONLY THE POWERS OF ALCHEMY CAN CAUSE ANY DAMAGE.

PAPILLON MASK PLANS TO ABANDON HIS SICK HUMAN BODY TO ATTAIN AN IMMORTAL HOMUNCULUS BODY!

"A HUMANOID HOMUNCULUS!"

YES, THAT WAS THE GOAL OF MY EXPERIMENTS. TO CREATE...

BUT ONCE YOU TAKE IN A HOMUNCULUS CORE...

I THOUGHT THE HUMAN SIDE OF YOU DIES...

YES, THE MIND IS KILLED AND IT TAKES OVER YOUR BODY.

BUT THERE'S ONE TYPE OF HOMUNCULUS THAT DOESN'T APPLY TO.

ON TOP OF THAT, MY BODY WILL BECOME THE CLOSEST THING TO BEING IMMORTAL.
THIS TWENTY FIRST CORE WAS CREATED USING MY CELLS AS A BASE! IT'S ME!
IF I MERGE WITH MY OWN SELF MY MIND WON'T BE KILLED.
A HUMANOID HOMUNCULUS WILL BE A SUPER HUMAN!
THE ANIMAL-TYPE AND PLANT-TYPE HOMUNCULI ARE MONSTERS BUT...
DO YOU REALLY WANT TO LIVE THAT BADLY?
YOU'VE ALREADY TAKEN COUNTLESS LIVES...
AND YOU PLAN TO TAKE EVEN MORE LIVES?
YOU'RE STILL A HOMUN-CULUS SO YOU'LL EAT PEOPLE RIGHT?
BUT ...

I TOLD YOU EARLIER. THE MOST IMPORTANT THING TO A PERSON IS THEIR LIFE.
I'LL DO ANYTHING TO STAY ALIVE.
I WANT TO LIVE.

IF YOU DON'T CARE ABOUT LIVING THEN WHY DIDN'T YOU STAY DEAD?
WHAT ABOUT YOU?
YOU'VE ALREADY DIED ONCE, RIGHT?

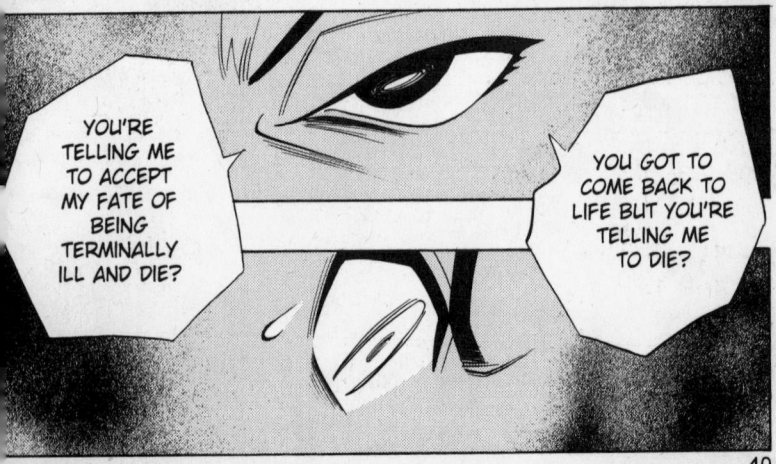
YOU'RE TELLING ME TO ACCEPT MY FATE OF BEING TERMINALLY ILL AND DIE?
YOU GOT TO COME BACK TO LIFE BUT YOU'RE TELLING ME TO DIE?

GO TO HELL.
!
THERE'S ONLY TWO MORE DAYS LEFT UNTIL IT'S FINISHED!
FWUP
!
NO!
ZA
THIS ENDS NOW!
I WON'T LET YOU BECOME A SUPER HUMAN!
THAT'S MY NEW LIFE!
I'M GOING TO USE IT TO MAKE THE TRANSFORMATION FROM A WORM TO A BUTTERFLY!

KAAW
!!!
THIS IS...
THIS POWER ...
HAWK HOMUN-CULUS!
THE LAST REMAINING ...

READ THIS WAY
!
SNAAGG
KRAK
KRIK
MAS-TER.
...ARE YOU ALL RIGHT?
KRRRASH

ALCHEMIC WARRIORS ...
HOW DARE YOU HARM MY MASTER!
LOOKS LIKE THE TABLES ARE TURNED!

NOW YOU'RE GOING TO TURN INTO A MONSTER AND DIE!
WHILE I'M GOING TO BECOME A SUPER HUMAN AND LIVE!
YOU WANT TO BECOME A MONSTER AND SUPER HUMAN...
I'M GOING TO MAKE SURE NEITHER HAPPENS!

- Height: 172cm; Weight: 62kg
- Born: August 8th; Leo; Blood type B; 16 years old
- Favorites: Ramen, The color black, cool motorcycles
- Dislikes: Gangs, people who litter cigarette butts
- Hobby: Touring on a 50cc scooter
- Things he's good at: Breaking tiles by head-butting them (?)
- Affiliation: Private Ginsei Academy 2nd Year High School Student
  Class Room B, Dorm resident

Character File No.9

Hideyuki Okakura

Author's Notes

- Another character created to liven up Kazuki's everyday life. He has the raised eyebrow look (the loud mouth) and he's also in charge of the joke puns.
- The more prominent one out of Kazuki's friends. Normally he's joking around with Kazuki but as an ex-delinquent he can throttle the enemy when necessary… was my initial concept but he somehow turned out to be the "So I'm controlled by passion! Damn it!" kind of guy.
- I based Hideyuki off an anime screenplay writer I went to Anime Expo with. (from my comments on the cover flap of Volume 1) He had so much character and was such a fun guy I thought if I brought his personality directly into the story he may overshadow the other characters so I ended up changing him quite a bit. But somehow, his "passionate" side stuck…

CHAPTER 10: VS. WASHIO: Section

Homunculus Overview

- The core is approximately 3cm and looks like a fetus. It will not survive for more than a day outside a small, enclosed space.
- Once it reaches the human brain, it overtakes the host's body and turns it into a monster that takes on traits of the base organism.

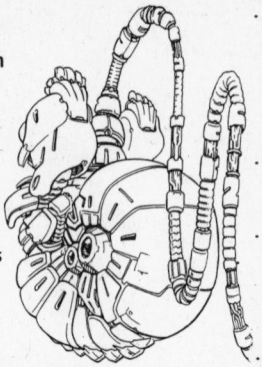

- The human's mind is killed and the mind of the base organism takes over. (i.e. – The animal/plant trait assimilates with human intelligence)
- Main diet is human but can feed off of other things. (The ultimate omnivore)
- Only the powers of Alchemy can destroy it. It's possible to inflict damage but will always regenerate. Close to being immortal.
- Homunculi are created using other organisms' cells as base.

VS. WASHIO: Section 1

Humanoid Homunculus

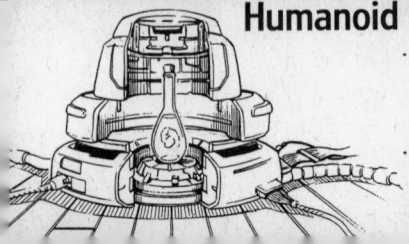

- A Homunculus that uses a human as its base enables the host to keep their mind but alters their body into being near immortal. Feeding on humans is unavoidable.
- By becoming a humanoid Homunculus Koushaku is planning to attain a new life. In two more days Koushaku's core will be complete.

YOU'RE ...
TELLING ME TO DIE TOO.
HUFF
HUFF
YOU'LL STOP ME...?
I SEE. MEANING ...
ZAH
YOU'RE WRONG!
I DON'T TELL PEOPLE TO DIE SO CALLOUSLY!
THERE'S NO TIME TO ARGUE.
PEOPLE WILL BE HERE SHORTLY.
MASTER, LEAVE THEM TO ME.
PLEASE RUN AWAY.
...AND LIVE TO THE FULLEST UNTIL YOU DIE!
YOU NEED TO MAKE IT UP TO THE PEOPLE THAT DIED...

WHAT HAPPENED?
WHAT THE HECK HAPPENED HERE?
RUSTLE
I SAW IT! IT WAS A METEOR!
RUSTLE
RUSTLE
LOOK
PEEK
WAS IT AN EXPLO-SION?
RUSTLE
HAS ANYONE CALLED THE POLICE OR THE FIRE DEPARTMENT?
CLASS LEADERS! TAKE A HEAD COUNT!
KAZUKI'S MISSING!
HE'S NOT HERE!
WHAT ...

I'LL HOLD OFF WASHIO!
TOKIKO, CAN YOU CATCH PAPILLON MASK?
SHOOM
WHAT?
MY LANCE IS FASTER WHEN CHARGING AT THE ENEMY.
FWO OOOO
IT'S ONLY A SECOND AT THIS DISTANCE!
...IN THE AIR THAT MIGHT NOT BE WISE BUT ON THE GROUND WITH SO MANY OBSTACLES AROUND, YOU MIGHT BE ABLE TO HIT BEFORE HE'S ABLE TO TRANSFORM.
OKAY!
LET'S DO IT!
BUSO ...
YOU'RE GOING TO...
CHALLENGE ME IN A CONTEST OF SPEED, EH...

!?!
FOR UNDER-ESTIMATING ME!!
FLASH
THIS IS WHAT YOU GET...

SO I CAN BECOME A HUMANOID HOMUNCULUS.
THEY WERE THE RESULTS OF MY ANIMAL EXPERIMENTS.
ALL THE CORES UNTIL NOW...
WERE MADE SO I CAN HAVE A NEW LIFE.
BUT THIS HAWK HOMUN-CULUS...
...IS EXTRA-ORDINARY.
WASHIO ...
?!
SCREECH

GLINT
WHOH
...WHAT'S HAPPENING? I'M GETTING ...
A BAD FEELING ...
CLENCH
WASH

HE'S A SELF-RIGHTEOUS HYPOCRITE.
I HATE PEOPLE LIKE THAT THE MOST.
YOU NEED TO MAKE IT UP TO THE PEOPLE THAT DIED...
...AND LIVE TO THE FULLEST UNTIL YOU DIE!
HMPH ...
...
TUP TUP
TWO MORE DAYS LEFT.
WHERE SHOULD I GO...
I'VE ...
LOST MY HOME AGAIN.

KABOOM
!!!!!!!!!!!!!!!!!!!
I CAN'T... BREATHE ...!
AT THIS... RATE... WE'RE GOING TO...!
MMM

I KNOW! LET'S DO IT!
TOKIKO!
BUSO RENKIN!

READ THIS WAY
!
THROB
PAM!!
!!

TOKIKO!
I'M... OKAY!
GIVE ME YOUR HAND!

READ THIS WAY
WAIT! LEAVE IT TO ME!
CHHHHH
GET READY TO LAND!
IT'S GOING TO BE DIFFICULT TO SUPPORT TWO PEOPLE'S WEIGHT WITH THE VALKYRIE SKIRT BUT I'LL TRY!
IT ACTIVATES AND TURNS INTO ENERGY WHEN IT RESONATES WITH MY WILL TO FIGHT!
GRIP
THE SPECIAL FEATURE ON MY BUSO RENKIN LANCE IS THIS CLOTH!
MY BUSO RENKIN !!!
BURST!

BOOM

VZT
VZT
TOK
HE DISSIPATED THE GRAVITATIONAL FORCE OF THE FALL USING THE CLOTH'S ENERGY...
HAH.
HAH.
HAH.
THAT WAS CLOSE.
PHEW
HIS BUSO RENKIN IS POWERFUL! SLOWLY BUT SURELY...
KAZUKI'S LEARNING TO MASTER HIS WEAPON!

YOU HAVE AMAZING POWERS ...
IMPRESSIVE, ALCHEMIC WARRIOR.
!!

READ THIS WAY
VIP
!!
FW 000 00
I GET IT... THIS TRANSFORMATION WILL ENABLE HIM TO MOVE MUCH FASTER.
HE'S ONLY TURNED A PORTION OF HIMSELF INTO A HOMUNCULUS!
I'VE NEVER SEEN THIS TYPE OF HOMUNCULUS!
HE'S DEFINITELY "EXTRAORDINARY" COMPARED TO THE OTHERS.
I'LL BE ABLE TO FIGHT AT FULL CAPACITY AGAINST YOU GUYS.
MY HEART TREMBLES WITH JOY!

- Height: 183cm; Weight: 85kg
- Born: September 14th; Virgo; Blood Type A; 16 years old
- Favorites: Coke, The color white, late night radio programs
- Dislikes: The eyes of broiled fish, gory horror films
- Hobby: Contributing to late night programs on the radio
- Things he's good at: Drawing, illustrating
- Affiliation: Private Ginsei Academy 2nd Year High School Student Class Room B, Dorm resident

Character File No.10

Masashi Daihama

Author's Notes

- Another character created to liven up Kazuki's everyday life. He has the curved eyebrow look (the Worrier) and he's also in charge of the joke puns.
- The laid-back one out of Kazuki's friends. He's usually running around backing up Kazuki and crew but as his name suggests he'll use his large body to protect his friends if necessary… was my initial concept but he somehow turned out to be the guy who's at the mercy of Kazuki's actions and always the most surprised.
- I based Daihama off an anime character designer I went to Anime Expo with. (from my comments on the cover flap of Volume 1). He's reserved but yet extremely talented. There's a Japanese proverb that describes him well: "A great hawk hides his claws." I wanted to incorporate that aspect into a character in my story so I borrowed his likeness.

CHAPTER 11: VS. WASHIO: Part 2: Section 1

GIGIGIG
SHOOM
I'LL CLIP YOUR WINGS!

I KNOW.
KPAAK
KSHHH
!!
WHAT?
IT'S TOO HARD ...
NO MATTER HOW FAST YOUR BLADES ARE IT'S IMPOSSIBLE TO CUT THROUGH IF THE BLADE DOESN'T STRIKE.

KREEEH
NNH!
ZASSH
!
KWWEEEN
BACK OFF, TOKIKO!

ENERGY!
FWA
A
SH
AT FULL CAPAC-ITY!
TAKE THIS!
JOUS-TING SLASH-ER!
WOO

NO! HE'S...
HE MISSED?
!!

TSS
TSS
LISTEN ...
NO MATTER HOW SHARP YOUR BLADES ARE, AS LONG AS I DISPLACE THE EDGE IT'S POSSIBLE TO DODGE IT.
DOOM
ONCE MORE!
ISSH!
TEAR HIM APART!
VSH!

HAK
YOU KNOW WHAT THIS IS?
IT'S CALLED, "READING THE ENEMY'S MOVE"...
I CAN ANTICIPATE YOUR SPEED.
VSS
VSS

SH
!
DAMN YOU!
KS
HAW

I WON'T LET YOU GET AWAY!
ROGER!
WE NEED TO REPOSITION OURSELVES!
LET'S RETREAT FOR NOW!
DSH
AGH!
JOUSTING FLASH!
VZZZ
LASH

...
PRETTY IMPRESSIVE ...
THEY'RE GOOD ON LAND AND QUICK THINKING.
ALSO THE GIRL ...
SHE'S SLIGHTLY SLOWER TODAY COMPARED TO WHEN I SAW HER LAUNCH AN ATTACK IN THE SKY.
THE BOY IS STILL INEXPERI-ENCED.
BUT ...
NO, I WILL WIN!
I CAN WIN!

FOR MASTER WHO GAVE ME THIS POWER!
WOOSH
HUFF.
HUFF.
HFF.
HFF.
STAND-BY MODE.
VALKYRIE SKIRT.
I DON'T KNOW WHAT'S SO IMPRESSIVE BUT...
YOU'LL BE ABLE TO DO A LOT MORE AS YOU GET MORE EXPERIENCE.
TUP TUP
WOW, THAT'S USEFUL!
THE VALKYRIE SKIRT IS IMPRESSIVE.

OH THAT?
IT'S MY SPECIAL ATTACKS!
IT'S EMBARRASSING LISTENING TO YOU.
WHY DO YOU KEEP DOING THAT?
ON ANOTHER NOTE, YOU'RE ALWAYS SCREAMING "SLASHER" OR "FLASHER" AND WHAT NOT.
DO YOU HAVE TO SCREAM TO DO IT?
IT GIVES YOU A DISADVANTAGE ...
BECAUSE YOU'RE TELLING THE ENEMY WHAT YOU'RE DOING.
NOT REALLY.
BUT I FEEL LIKE IT'LL BE MORE EFFECTIVE IF I YELL IT OUT.
YOUR GUTS!
I'LL SPLATTER ...
...I SEE. MAKES SENSE.
RIGHT?
ANYWAY, WIPE THE BLOOD OFF. A BLOODY SMILE IS A BIT SCARY.
THANKS. ARE YOU OKAY TOKIKO?
MY RIGHT SHOULDER IS A BIT...
SS

READ THIS WAY
TOKIKO?
NO, I'M FINE. IT'S NO BIG DEAL.
DON'T PUSH YOURSELF TOO HARD.
LOOK WHO'S TALKING.
WHO DO YOU THINK I AM?
AN ALCHEMIC WARRIOR WHO'S STRONGER THAN ME.
REALLY ...
BUT I HAVE TO SAY IT.
THESE THINGS HAVE TO BE SAID.
OKAY.
I'LL BE CAREFUL.

HIS DEFENSE USING HIS WINGS ISN'T A SKILL THAT COMES NATURALLY.
HE DIDN'T BECOME OVERCONFIDENT IN HIS POWERS. HE STUDIED THE ART OF FIGHTING AND TRAINED HARD TO ACQUIRE THAT SKILL.
THAT HAWK HOMUNCULUS ...
IT'S OBVIOUSLY SUPERIOR COMPARED TO THE OTHER HOMUNCULI.
BUT ...
WE'RE IN THE MIDST OF BATTLE.
DON'T GET ME WRONG. I'M SAYING HE'S A MONSTER THAT'S MUCH MORE DISCIPLINED THAN THE ORDINARY HOMUNCULUS.
SO THAT HAWK GUY IS A HOMUNCULUS WARRIOR?
AS LONG AS HE'S A MONSTER THERE'S ALWAYS A WAY...
TO DESTROY HIM!

READ THIS WAY
HE'S COMING!
KA
KA
KA
I FOUND YOU!
THERE'S ONLY ONE! THEY MUST'VE SPLIT INTO TWO GROUPS!!

THE HAWK'S WING DEFENSE IS GREAT BUT IT'S NOT FOOL-PROOF!
OKAY, KAZUKI.

OUR PLAN IS TO LAUNCH A ONE-SHOT HIGH-SPEED MULTIPLE ATTACK!
DM DM DM DM DM
HE CAN'T DEFEND HIMSELF USING HIS WINGS AGAINST A MULTIPLE ATTACK.
HE USED HIS CLAWS WHEN WE ATTACKED HIM AT THE SAME TIME.

WILL LAUNCH A POWERFUL ATTACK!
VOOOM
ONE OF US WILL ACT AS A DECOY AND ATTACK. AFTER HE USES HIS WINGS TO DEFEND HIMSELF, THE OTHER ...

OKAY!
I'LL BE THE DECOY!

TO HIDE TOKIKO UNTIL THE LAST MINUTE!
WITH MY LANCE I CAN COMBINE THE SLASHER AND FLASHER SKILLS...
SHEEEN
I'M COMING FOR YOU!
VOO
GH
...

Liner Notes #8 ~ #11 (1)

Chapter 8: Lock on

· This was the first chapter where there were no battles so I experimented a lot with comedic elements. The funny faces I drew were very popular. (Kazuki is a big fan of Rohan Kishibe.)

· I introduced Tokiko's background a little. I wanted to keep her the "mysterious girl" a little longer but due to the unexpected high volume of questions I inserted a little information. Tokiko is still the most popular character. You can do it Kazuki!

· Koushaku officially makes his grand entrance. I wasn't sure how I felt about him saying "Kazuki's right" for a punchline as he's supposed to be the boss character but I figured this chapter had a lot of comedy in it so I went with it. In the end, I think these words added to the type of character Papillon would be later on.

Chapter 9: The Other New Life

· Koushaku's true intentions are revealed. It's becoming more Alchemic-like with the immortality theme… I think?

· I laid out the "So, what do you say?" line like that to make it more impressionable. Normally I don't really think about matching the lips to the lines but after I got an understanding from doing this, I think I've gotten a little better at drawing the subtle facial expressions.

Chapter 10: VS. Washio: Section 1

· "Everything's in place! Time for battle!" As such, I was really pumped but the next four chapters ended up being extremely unpopular… Looking back, I could understand where people were coming from. I was honestly upset during this incident.

· I used a lot of large frames to capture the action but the content ended up being thin. It also didn't help that the previous episodes were full of content so when you read through it, it felt even thinner… (Factor 1)

· There are two reasons for Washio's partial transformation. I wanted to show he was different from the others and I also wanted to ease the amount of work put into drawing him. The reason why his wings are growing out of his arms is because I hate the "angel" design with a passion. Enough with the girls with swan wings on her back… I figured the appeal of unconventional beauty comes from "The Beauty found in the Ugly" or "The Ugly found in the Beauty?"

Chapter 11: VS. Washio: Part 2: Section 1

· "What the heck is Section 1?" I got that question A LOT. I even questioned it myself. Even my editor said "Maybe we should amend it in the tankoban?" but I decided to keep it as a reminder to myself, although embarrassing.

· I'm sure you've realized this but the VS. Washio chapters were supposed to end in three chapters. Once I started drawing, I realized how difficult the action scenes were to draw. It took a lot of work to make sure Washio's claws, wings and Kazuki's giant lance fit within the frame.

Continued on page 106

CHAPTER 12: VS. WASHIO: Part 2: Section 2

DID YOU FIND KAZUKI?
NO, HE'S NOT HERE!
HE'S NOT AT THE SCHOOL EITHER!

APPARENTLY HE WAS SEEING TOKIKO BEFORE MEETING UP WITH US.
TOK
WHAT? THEN HE'S...!

YEAH, HE'S BEEN DISAPPEARING A LOT SINCE SHE CAME INTO THE PICTURE.
GLAD TO HEAR HE'S OKAY THOUGH.
DAMN IT! HE'S GOING TO GET IT TONIGHT!

I HAVE A BAD FEELING ...
I FEEL LIKE I'M NEVER GOING TO SEE BROTHER AND TOKIKO...
EVER AGAIN ...

DABOOM
OUR PLAN IS TO LAUNCH A ONE-SHOT HIGH-SPEED MULTIPLE ATTACK!

ONE OF US WILL ACT AS A DECOY AND ATTACK TO MAKE HIM USE HIS WINGS TO DEFEND HIMSELF.
I'M COMING FOR YOU!
AFTER HE SHIFTS HIS POSITION TO BLOCK IT, THE OTHER WILL LAUNCH A POWERFUL ATTACK!
HIDE IN THE LIGHT AND FOLLOW ME! TOKIKO!
WHOOM

READ THIS WAY
ACTI-VATE!
VALKYRIE SKIRT.
...SUCH A BEAUTIFUL GOLDEN YELLOW LIGHT.
IT'S LIKE THE RAYS OF THE SUN...
!!

URAAAHH!
VROOSHH
SHEEN
FWOOO

IT'S FAINT BUT I CAN FEEL A SEPARATE WIND.
THIS WIND IS DIFFERENT FROM THE ONE BEFORE.
?
NO.
HE'S NOT JUST USING HIS EYES. HE'S READING THE WIND FLOW...
!!
GRRRRRRR
I'LL TAKE CARE OF BOTH OF YOU WITH MY CLAWS!
I GOT IT! THE GIRL IS BEHIND THE LIGHT!

WE FAILED! RUN TOKIKO!
DAMN IT!
GSSHHH
DSSSSH
DON'T STOP KAZUKI.
DOGUSSH

HH
HOW COULD I HAVE LET YOU GET ABOVE ME TWICE!
I WON'T LOSE!
I'LL SPLATTER ...
HHHH
YOUR GUTS!
!

TOKIKO!
SHO
OMI
...ZUKI...
KA...
NOW!
PIERCE THROUGH HIM!
KYAA

JOUSTING SLASHER!
UR ...
AHHHH!

TOKIKO!
WHY DID YOU ...
BECAUSE HE SAW THROUGH OUR PLAN... SO I CHANGED IT.
BUT ...!
KSHINK

THIS IS PROBABLY THE LAST TIME I CAN REALLY FIGHT.
SWUP
PLUS ...
THAT'S WHAT WAS GOING THROUGH MY MIND WHEN I ATTACKED BUT...
I COULDN'T FAIL.
I'M STARTING TO LOSE CONTROL OF MY BODY.
IT'S FINALLY REACHED MY SPINAL CORD...
HAA
HAA

BAM
WHAT A DANGEROUS WOMAN...
YOUR VENGEFULNESS WILL SURELY THREATEN MASTER EVEN AFTER YOU'VE BECOME A HOMUNCULUS.
HAA
HAA
VZZZ
I MUST FINISH YOU OFF NOW!
LOOKS LIKE HE NEEDS A FINAL BLOW ...
ZAM
PAT

!
VEEEEN
LEAVE THE REST TO ME.
I WANT YOU TO REST.
GRAB
FROM HERE ON...
I'LL FIGHT ALONE.

...DESTROY THE TWENTY-FIRST CORE AND...
GET THE ANTIDOTE!
FWWW
WWW
I'LL DESTROY HIM...
...CATCH PAPILLON...
I KNOW THAT USUALLY THE DECOY IS THE WEAKER FIGHTER...
IT'S USELESS TO ACT TOUGH.
I NEED TO KILL THE GIRL FIRST.
I'LL DEAL WITH YOU AFTERWARDS.
I'M NOT MOVING!
BACK OFF!

MOVE!!
DS
SHH
!

READ THIS WAY
RIGHT NOW, YOU'RE NO MATCH FOR HIM!
BACK OFF KAZUKI!
I'M NOT BACKING DOWN! EVEN IF IT'S AN ORDER....
I'M NOT BACKING DOWN NO MATTER WHAT!
KA
KRE
SSH

- (Continued from page 86) Even if I managed to fit it, the frames ended up being bigger than I thought. That's why the page count got bigger and the content got even thinner. (Factor 2)
- Kazuki's line where he says, "I feel like it'll be more effective if I yell it out" is my own comical question to my manga and to all other Battle Manga where they always announce their attack. Although in its defense, it's been proven that being vocal has a positive effect in The Hammer Throw and Weight Lifting sports.

Chapter 12: VS. Washio: Part 2: Section 2

- "What the heck is Section 2?" I got that question A LOT.
- In this chapter I continued to agonize over how to draw the battle scenes and became hesitant at times.
- Kazuki hasn't learned how to properly fight so he only has forward attacks. Washio's claws and wings are too big so it's hard to grasp what it is as a whole. Tokiko's Valkyrie Skirt is too robotic and difficult to draw in hand-to-hand combat scenes. I completely missed the above points. A lot of other things that I didn't even consider came up too. They look great by themselves but I can't manipulate them well when I combine them. (Factor 3)
- Tokiko's spine drawings were both popular and unpopular as people thought it looked painful. It's difficult to draw something that conveys pain so I'm pretty happy about this one.

Chapter 13: VS. Washio: Part 3

- Finally, the last segment.
- This chapter touches upon Washio's background. In the end where Tokiko says, "...it's instinctual for an animal to fear death but yet he put his life..." I wanted to draw the irony in what Washio was saying more dramatically but at this point I couldn't make a Section 3 so I opted not to reluctantly.
- The battle scenes were lacking contextual depth until the very end. Hmm... It's an important factor to consider moving forward.

Chapter 14: Midnight Run 2

- In the beginning I planned Kazuki to take Tokiko to the Koushaku family estate with him and settle the score. After the battle he would return to the dorm as the sun rose. Mahiro would notice a change in Kazuki as Kazuki had awakened as a Warrior and was no longer an ordinary high school student. Mahiro's "bad feeling" in Chapter 12 was actually leading up to this storyline.
- Learning my lesson from the unpopular VS. Washio chapters I decided to change it. My editor at the time and I discussed and came to the conclusion that "the readers weren't ready to have Kazuki part from his ordinary life. Perhaps the readers had their expectations betrayed by having Kazuki taken away from that to fight Washio in the mountains?" (Factor 4) That's why I decided to change the story progression by incorporating "ordinary life, meaning Mahiro and the three guys at the dorm."
- I changed Mahiro's character to be the space cadet character.
- I threw out an entire side story, changed the progression and altered a character. After doing everything I can to make it more interesting, it finally got back the popularity level before the VS. Washio chapters. I learned a very valuable lesson.

CHAPTER 13: VS. WASHIO: Part 3

SHWAK

WHAK

CHAPTER 13:

VS. WASHIO: Part 3

FWIP
SLASH-ER!
WOOM
JOUS TING ...
CLA NK
I READ THE WIND WITH MY WINGS.
IT'S USELESS NO MATTER HOW MANY TIMES YOU TRY.
I MISSED AGAIN!
IT DIDN'T WORK!

NO MATTER THE SITUATION, MY WINGS WILL NOT FAIL TO PROTECT ME!
BASH
BEFORE I SEE IT WITH MY EYES AND HEAR IT WITH MY EARS, THE WIND ACCURATELY TELLS ME EVERYTHING!
!
DG DG DG DG DG
HE'S INEXPERIENCED.
HIS WIND HAS CHANGED SLIGHTLY.
HIS WIND IS FAR FROM BEING FIERCE OR VIOLENT...
GRAB
BUT ...

HUF
A STRONG...
HUF
HUF
HUF
BUT I FEEL...
BREATH OF LIFE.
HUF
HUF
THE REASON MUST BE...
PEEK
HIS GUARD IS STILL SOLID EVEN IF HE HAS ONLY ONE WING LEFT...
THIS HOMUNCULUS.
KAZUKI CAN'T HANDLE HIM ALONE...
WE NEED TO TAKE HIS GUARD DOWN AND FINISH HIM OFF.
SWUP
HAA
HAA

TOKIKO, I WANT YOU TO STAY OUT OF IT.
DSSSH
HERE I COME!

READ THIS WAY
IS SHE THAT IMPORTANT TO YOU?
THAT GIRL ...
OR ARE YOU TWO A COUPLE?
?
IS YOUR POWER DETERMINED BY STRENGTH?
?!
I FEEL WEIRD NOT ANSWERING WHEN HE ASKS A QUESTION. I FEEL SORT OF...
BUT ...
RUDE?
YOU'RE IN THE MIDDLE OF A BATTLE KAZUKI!
IGNORE HIM!
THEN BE RUDE!

I DIED ONCE...
BUT SHE GAVE ME A NEW LIFE AND ALCHEMIC POWERS.
!
I OWE MY LIFE TO TOKIKO.

KYA
I CAN'T LOSE!
AND NOW HER LIFE IS ON THE LINE!

HUH?

UNBELIEVABLE. WE'RE THE SAME.

MY LIFE TO MASTER.
I OWE ...

HAWKS ARE THE LARGEST PREDATOR. WE RULE THE SKIES.
I WAS THE MIGHTIEST OF THE HAWKS.
BOOM
BUT...
AND DIED.
I FELL...
I WAS MISTAKENLY SHOT OR HUNTED.
THAT'S ALL IT TAKES.
BEFORE I HAD THIS BODY I WAS A WILD HAWK.

YOU AND I ARE BOTH IN LUCK.
BE HAPPY. I'LL BRING YOU BACK TO LIFE.
GRIN
I CAME TO GET BUTTERFLIES SO I WASN'T EXPECTING TO BE ABLE TO GET A HOLD OF SOMETHING SO RARE.
AN UNTIMELY DEATH CAN COME FOR EVEN A NATIONAL TREASURE.
BUT I GUESS THAT'S LIFE.
RESURRECTED.
I WAS ...
I DIED ONCE...
BUT HE GAVE ME A NEW LIFE AND POWERS.
I OWE MY LIFE TO MASTER.
I WON'T ALLOW YOU TO STAND IN HIS WAY!
HIS LIFE IS ON THE LINE RIGHT NOW!
HYAA

READ THIS WAY
HIS HEIGHTENED AWARENESS OF BATTLES COMES FROM THE INSTINCTS OF A WILD ANIMAL.
NO WONDER ...
HIS UNUSUAL LEVEL OF LOYALTY ISN'T FROM BEING "BRAINWASHED." SO THAT'S WHY...
THE ONES WE OWE OUR LIVES TO ARE DIFFERENT!
I SEE, SO WE'RE THE SAME.
BUT ...
SHE EVEN PRAYED FOR THE PEOPLE WHO DIED.
SHE WAS EVEN CONCERNED FOR MAHIRO.
TOKIKO GAVE ME THE KAKUGANE BECAUSE SHE WAS CONCERNED ABOUT ME.
HE FEARS DEATH SO MUCH HE'S ONLY CONCERNED ABOUT SURVIVAL.
HE COULD CARE LESS ABOUT OTHER PEOPLE'S LIVES.
PAPILLON... KOUSHAKU ONLY VIEWS YOU GUYS AS GUINEA PIGS.
I DON'T WANT TOKIKO TO DIE FROM SOMEONE LIKE THAT! THAT'S WHY I...
UHH...
WHAT KOUSHAKU IS DOING IS WRONG!

GAH!
I DON'T CARE!
KAZU-KI!
I KNOW THAT ALL TOO WELL AS I LIVED IN THE WILD.
SLIP
IT'S INSTINCTUAL FOR AN ANIMAL TO "FEAR DEATH."
MASTER'S ACTIONS AREN'T A MISTAKE!

ABOUT FEARING DEATH OR FLEEING FROM IT.
THERE'S NOTHING SHAMEFUL OR EVIL...
IF YOU SWEAR TO STAY AWAY FROM MASTER AND FORFEIT...
I'LL LET YOU GO AND LET YOU LIVE.
I HONESTLY DOUBT YOU WANT TO DIE LIKE THIS EITHER...
DOOM
BUT THERE'S SOMEONE WHO WILL DEFINITELY DIE IF I RUN AWAY.
CLENCH
!
I WILL NOT LOSE!
I REFUSE TO BACK DOWN.

I REFUSE TO LET TOKIKO DIE!
HUFF
HUFF
!!
HE'S WRAPPED THE CLOTH AROUND HIS LANCE!
THE CLOTH'S ENERGY ENHANCES HIS SPEED AND ALSO ADDS TO THE LANCE'S DESTRUCTIVE FORCE!!
BUT ...
YOU'RE RIGHT.
I'M SCARED OF DYING ...

READ THIS WAY
BUT BOTH KOUSHAKU AND I ARE HUMAN.
I KNOW WHAT DEATH IS LIKE BECAUSE I'VE DIED BEFORE. I THINK PAPILLON... KOUSHAKU KNOWS THAT AS WELL BECAUSE HE'S ON THE VERGE OF DEATH HIMSELF.
THERE ARE THINGS THAT WE SHOULDN'T DO EVEN IF IT MEANS DEATH...
THAT'S WHY ...
EVEN IF IT KILLS US!
AND THERE ARE THINGS THAT WE NEED TO DO...
STOP KAZUKI!
HE'S HURTING HIMSELF!
!!

JOUSTING
AT FULL CAPAC-ITY!
ENERGY ...

READ THIS WAY
CRACK
CRACK
CRACK
CRACK
CRASHER!!
THE BREATH OF LIFE ...
TURNED INTO THE... WIND...

I'M GLAD TO HEAR THAT... NOW I CAN DIE IN PEACE...
HUF
I NEVER PLANNED TO.
I'M NOT GOING TO KILL HIM.
HUF
HUF
I'M JUST GOING TO STOP HIM.
I KNOW THIS IS SELFISH... OF ME BUT...
I NEED TO... ASK YOU... A FAVOR...
SHUUUU...
MY MASTER ...
I DIDN'T KNOW... THERE... WAS SUCH...
DIE IN... PEACE... EH?
A DEATH ...

HE WAS A DIFFERENT TYPE OF HOMUNCULUS EVEN IN DEATH AND THIS WAS A VALUABLE EXPERIENCE FOR YOU.
IT'S TRULY RARE THAT SOMEONE COULD USE THEIR BUSO RENKIN SO WELL IN ONE WEEK...
AMEN.
NAMU AMI DABUTSU.
HE SAID IT'S INSTINCTUAL FOR AN ANIMAL TO FEAR DEATH, YET HE PUT HIS LIFE ON THE LINE AND FOUGHT TO PROTECT PAPILLON ...

WE HAVE UNTIL TWELVE O'CLOCK MIDNIGHT TOMORROW...
THERE'S ONLY ONE MORE DAY LEFT...
THE FIFTH DAY IS ENDING.

I WANT YOU TO LISTEN CARE-FULLY.

YOU CAN'T IN THAT CONDI-TION.
WE'RE SPENDING THE NIGHT HERE.
THERE'S SOMETHING I NEED TO TALK TO YOU ABOUT.

ARE YOU OKAY TOKIKO?
LET'S CLIMB DOWN THE MOUNTAIN BEFORE IT GETS DARK ...
HUF
FWIP
HUF

Character File No.11

Homunculus Washio

- Height: 195cm; Weight: 90kg
- Born: January 10th; Capricorn; Blood Type A; 25 years old
  Above is an assumption of his human form
- Favorites: Rabbits (yummy), the will to fight for survival
- Dislikes: Any threat to the Creator, hunting rifles, unnecessary battles
- Hobby: Flying around
- Things he's good at: Partial transformation into a Homunculus.

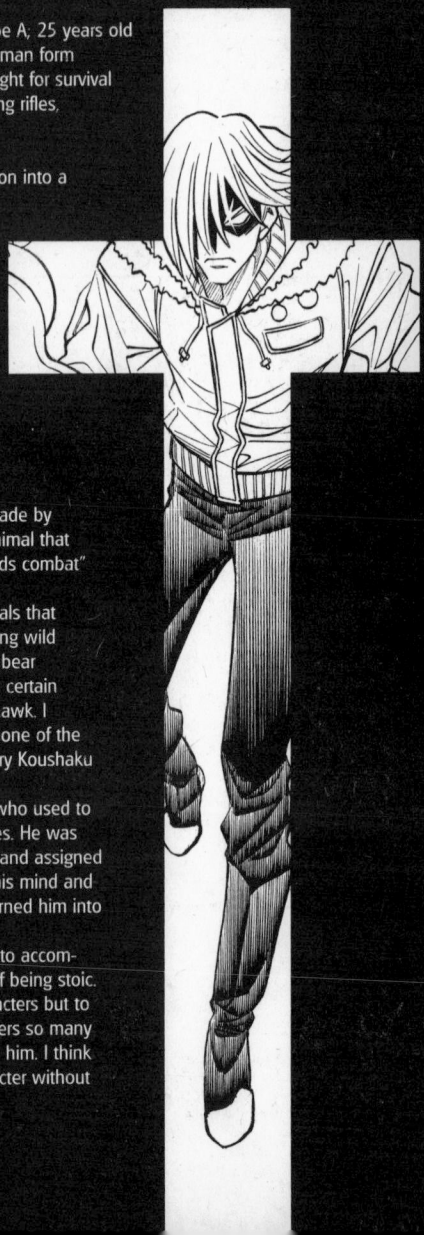

Author's Notes

- As the most powerful Homunculus made by Koushaku, it needed to be "a wild animal that has a strong affinity and talent towards combat" so I put some thoughts into it.
- Hawks and bears were the two animals that came to mind when I thought of strong wild animals that live in Japan. I figured a bear would be too similar to Saruwatari in certain respects so instead I went with the hawk. I figured it would have speed, which none of the other Homunculi have, and could carry Koushaku who's sick.
- Originally he was a Yakuza member who used to be a soldier in the Self-Defense Forces. He was sent to work at the Koushaku family and assigned as Koushaku's trainer to strengthen his mind and body. Koushaku resented him and turned him into a Homunculus.
- He is extremely loyal and committed to accomplishing a goal, almost to the point of being stoic. I've always liked these types of characters but to be honest, I've drawn similar characters so many times before, I really couldn't get into him. I think he turned out really good for a character without a design motif but…

CHAPTER 14:

MIDNIGHT RUN 2

I HAVE AN IDEA WHERE HE'D BE.
KLIK
IT'S ALMOST LIKE A FULL DAY'S TREK.
THEN AS SOON AS WE ARRIVE WE HAVE TO FIND KOUSHAKU.

THE LAST PLACE HE CAN GO TO HIDE IS WITH HIS FAMILY. HE'S PROBABLY AT HIS HOUSE.
HE'S NOT STRONG AND HE HAS NO FRIENDS.
NOW THAT ALL OF HIS HOMUNCULUS ARE LOST, HE'S JUST A NORMAL HIGH SCHOOL KID.

I'M STAYING HERE.
YES, THAT'S WHY I'M LEAVING THE REST TO YOU AND...
OKAY!
WE HAVE UNTIL MIDNIGHT TOMORROW!
CLENCH
WE HAVE TONS OF TIME!

SHAKE
HEY! STOP SHAKING ME!
SHAKE
SHAKE
WE'RE BOTH AT THE BRINK OF EXHAUSTION!
WE STILL HAVE TIME TO MAKE IT!
WHAT ARE YOU TALKING ABOUT?
YOU'RE NOT MAKING ANY SENSE!
SHAKE
SHAKE
SHAKE
I SAID STOP...!
HFF
HFF
HFF
TWITCH
TWITCH
HFF
HFF
HFF
WE'LL ONLY MAKE IT IF IT'S JUST YOU.
THANKS TO THIS...
MY LEGS ARE PARALYZED. I CAN'T MOVE.
SW
I CAN'T GET OFF THIS MOUNTAIN.
BUT EVEN IF I GET THE ANTIDOTE THERE WON'T BE ENOUGH TIME TO BRING IT TO YOU...
IT'S FINE.
THERE'S NO NEED TO COME BACK.

ONCE YOU LEAVE TOMORROW MORNING AND AFTER I LOSE SIGHT OF YOU...
I'LL FINISH MYSELF OFF.
SHAKE
I SAID, STOP SHAKING ME!
SHAKE
THERE HAS TO BE A WAY!
WHY ARE YOU GIVING UP!
WE'RE BOTH GONNA DIE AT THIS RATE!
YOU CAN'T DIE!
I'M SERIOUS. STOP IT...!
SHAKE
SHAKE
SHAKE
HFF
HFF
HFF
TWITCH
TWITCH
HFF
HFF
HFF
YOU WERE TELLING ME THIS MORNING THAT THERE'S A "MAIN SQUAD"!
THE "MAIN SQUAD!"
WE CAN ASK THEM FOR EMERGENCY ASSISTANCE!
HUH?
THAT'S IT!
FWUP

UNFORTUNATELY, EVEN IF WE REQUEST EMERGENCY ASSISTANCE, THERE'S NO WAY THEY CAN HELP BEFORE MIDNIGHT TOMORROW.
IT'S NO USE. ALL THE WARRIORS IN JAPAN ARE ON ACTIVE DUTY.
FWP
FWP
I'VE BEEN GIVING THEM PERIODIC REPORTS SO I'M SURE THEY'LL TAKE SOME SORT OF ACTION BUT THAT IS AFTER THEY ASSESS THE ENTIRE SITUATION ...

WILL COME BEFORE YOU.
AFTER THAT... IT SHOULDN'T TAKE THEM LONG.
KAZUKI, ANOTHER WARRIOR...

FORGET EVERYTHING THAT HAS HAPPENED IN THE LAST WEEK.
AFTER YOU REPORT EVERYTHING TO THEM FOR ME...

AS LONG AS YOU PROMISE TO NEVER USE THE BUSO RENKIN I DOUBT THE MAIN SQUAD WILL TAKE YOU INTO CUSTODY.
THE KAKUGANE IS PRECIOUS AND VERY FEW EXIST BUT...
AS LONG AS THE MAIN SQUAD KNOWS ITS LOCATION AND THAT IT WON'T BE USED FOR EVIL THEY SHOULD BE OKAY.
YOU SHOULD RETURN TO YOUR NORMAL LIFE.
SPENDING TIME WITH YOUR SISTER AND FRIENDS SUITS YOU BETTER.
Fwwooo
HUH?
RIGHT NOW.
GOOD.
OKAY. I'LL GO HOME.

HEEEEY!
DADADADA
DADADA
DON'T TAKE ADVANTAGE OF THE SITUATION JUST BECAUSE I CAN'T MOVE!
IF WE GET OFF THE MOUNTAIN BEFORE SUNRISE...
WE SHOULD BE ABLE TO MAKE IT BACK BY TOMORROW AFTERNOON!
IT'S OKAY! YOU'RE REALLY LIGHT!
YOU'RE PUSHING YOURSELF TOO HARD! YOU'RE GOING TO COLLAPSE FROM EXHAUSTION!
YOU IDIOT! THAT'S NOT THE POINT!

TOOM TOOM TOOM TOOM
PLEASE PUT ME DOWN!
NO WAY!
I SAID PUT ME DOWN!!
PUT ME DOWN!
NO!
NOPE!

YOU'RE ONE OF THOSE PEOPLE TOO, TOKIKO!
I TOLD YOU. I WON'T LET ANYONE ELSE DIE!

I SWEAR WE *WILL* MAKE IT!
TUP
WE CAN MAKE IT!

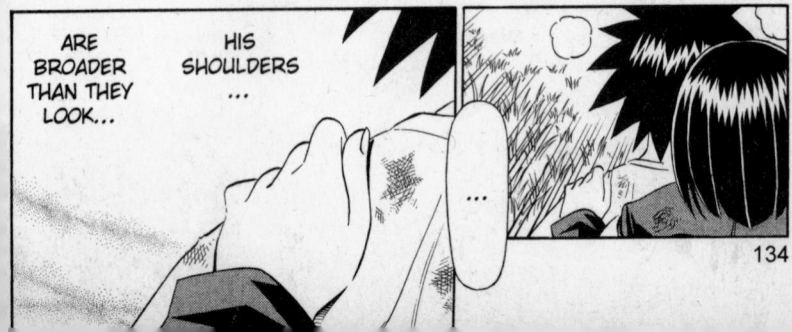
ARE BROADER THAN THEY LOOK...
HIS SHOULDERS ...
...

CONTINUING WITH OUR NEWS REPORT ...
HE'S BEEN DISAP-PEARING A LOT LATELY BUT HE'S NEVER BEEN GONE FOR A FULL DAY ...
KAZUKI HASN'T COME HOME YET...
A STRONG WIND GUST OF UNKNOWN ORIGIN DESTROYED...
THE INCIDENT THAT OCCURRED AT GINSEI ACADEMY, HIGH SCHOOL DORMITORY IN GINSEI CITY, SAITAMA PREFECTURE ...
SONY

HEY. I'M KAZUKI.
WHO ARE YOU REALLY?!
TAP
TAP
YOU DID?!
HE'S LUCKY I FAKED HIS VOICE AND COVERED FOR HIM WHEN THEY WERE TAKING HEAD COUNT LAST NIGHT.
YEAH.
HIS USUAL QUIRKY BEHAVIORS GOT A TURBO BOOST!
ANYWAY, EVER SINCE TOKIKO CAME INTO THE PICTURE ...
IF HE WAS...
DO YOU THINK HE'S IN SOME KIND OF TROUBLE?
BROTHER ...
TOK

...
I'M HOME ...
HEAVE
HEAVE
!
KAZU-KI!
BRO-THER!
DASH
LOVEY-DOVEY PLUS TATTERED AND TORN?!
I'M BEGGING YOU. PLEASE PUT ME DOWN...
GET BLOWN AWAY BY YESTERDAY'S WIND GUST?
DID YOU ...
WHAT HAPPENED?

TOKIKO SLIPPED A DISC IN HER BACK. IT HAPPENS EVERY SO OFTEN AND SHE CAN'T MOVE WHEN IT DOES.
THAT'S WHY I PIGGYBACKED HER ALL THE WAY HERE.
SNAP
YEAH! THAT!
I CARRIED HER ON PIGGYBACK ALL THE WAY.
IN THE PACKED TRAIN, MAIN ROADS AND EVEN THROUGH THE SHOPPING DISTRICT
...
YUP. ALL THE WAY.
ALL THE WAY?
HE'S RIGHT TOKIKO! A SLIPPED DISC IS CURABLE!
SHE'S GULLIBLE... SHE'S DEFINITELY KAZUKI'S SISTER.
IT'S TOO EARLY TO GIVE UP!
NO WHINING ALLOWED!
THAT'S ENOUGH.
I'VE HAD ENOUGH SO...
PUT ME OUT OF MY MISERY ...
LO M

NO, IT HAS TO BE DONE TONIGHT.
YEAH, THERE'S SOMETHING I STILL NEED TO DO.
WAIT A SEC. YOU'RE LEAVING AGAIN?
GRAB
BUT YOU'RE TORN UP. YOU SHOULD REST TODAY AND DO IT TOMORROW.
OKAY, I HAVE TO GET GOING.
WHAT!
I NEED YOU TO LOOK AFTER TOKIKO!
GRAB
HUH?
THAT'S WHY... MAHIRO, WHILE I'M GONE...
PLEASE!
I'LL BE BACK AS SOON AS I CAN!

WAIT, KAZUKI.
I'M A MASTER NURSE!
THERE'S NO POINT IN HIDING IT NOW!
OKAY! LEAVE IT TO ME!
IT'S A KAZUKI.
A FEMALE KAZUKI...
DA

ARE YOU IN SOME KIND OF TROUBLE?
ARE YOU HIDING SOMETHING FROM US?

I'M IN A TIGHT SPOT RIGHT NOW.
...I'M SORRY. OKAKURA, YOU'RE RIGHT.

SO I'LL BE FINE!
BUT IT'LL ALL BE SOLVED TONIGHT
CLEVER!
NO WORRIES, NO PROBLEM, EH?
I WAS PLANNING TO HELP EVEN IF YOU COULDN'T TELL ME THE DETAILS BUT...
LEAVE TOKIKO TO ME!
THEN HURRY UP AND GO SOLVE IT!
I'LL FAKE YOUR VOICE AND COVER FOR YOU WHEN THEY TAKE HEAD COUNT AGAIN!
ONE MORE RUN!
DASH
ALL RIGHT!

TAKE THIS WITH YOU.
WHOA, YOU'RE RIGHT!
TP
YOUR CELL IS BROKEN FROM LAST NIGHT'S BATTLE.
MAKE SURE YOU REPORT AS OFTEN AS YOU CAN.
WAIT KAZUKI.
IF NECESSARY, YOU CAN USE ONE AS A BUSO RENKIN AND THE OTHER TO HEAL YOU. IT WILL EASE THE BURDEN ON YOUR BODY EVEN DURING BATTLE.
XLIV
IT WON'T DOUBLE YOUR STRENGTH BUT TWO WILL HEAL YOU FASTER THAN ONE.
AND TAKE THIS.
INSTEAD OF DOING IT FOR ME...
KAZUKI, I SAID THIS BEFORE BUT YOU'RE BETTER OFF WITH YOUR SISTER AND YOUR FRIENDS. BATTLE DOESN'T SUIT YOU.
I WILL!
ROGER!
MAKE SURE YOU COME BACK!
DO IT FOR YOUR-SELF!

FWWWWW
I'M HERE!
THIS IS KOUSHAKU'S HOUSE!
SAY
FIVE HOURS LEFT...
BLB
MIDNIGHT.
THE TIME LIMIT IS...
ONLY FIVE MORE HOURS UNTIL I GET MY NEW LIFE!

Liner Notes #15 ~ 17

Chapter 15: Dark, Hot and Sweet

- Nurse Mahiro and Shishio Tokiko... I'm sorry. It's not the characters that are going out of control. It's me.
- I got the idea of the transformation scene in his underwear from *Devilman's* transformation scene and Santana from Part 2 in *Jojo's Bizarre Adventure*. No need to accessorize excessively! If you're Super Human show off that body! ...is what I thought but thinking I might have gone overboard I spoke to Kurosaki Sensei for advice. He said, "If you think it's interesting do it!" Those were very encouraging words. It's an understatement to stay the Papillon character was finalized from those words.
- Koushaku's lines describing human flesh came from Talleyrand, a French foreign minister. That's what he said when he described good coffee. I'd like to have some of the coffee he was having.

Chapter 16: Butterfly of Black Death

- This was the most cumbersome chapter of this volume. Seems like a lot of people were confused not knowing whether this chapter was serious or comedic. To be honest, I really don't know myself. I just know I had a lot of fun drawing it. I felt the "rush" a lot in this chapter. It's that feeling you get only in sequential manga. This is why I can't give up manga.
- I had thought of the Double Buso Renkin before the series started. Power-Ups are a part of the thrill of Shonen Manga but I thought it would be weird if he suddenly got stronger. I also didn't want him to get stronger with me unconvinced. That's why he ended up defeating Koushaku by borrowing Tokiko's power but it was all Kazuki.
- I got the second lance's design motif from *Getter Robo*. I LOVE *GETTER*.

Chapter 17: Fade to Black

- The four action pages. I learned from my mistake from the VS. Washio chapters. I omitted everything unnecessary and drew it to convey a sense of speed. It might look like a one shot drawing using ink but actually a lot of effort was put into drawing these pages.
- The scene where Kazuki says he's "sorry" and the part where Koushaku says, "don't apologize" is my favorite scene in the entire volume. It's very difficult to really sense the various emotions going through them with just words but these scenes are the most fulfilling to draw.
- The Warrior Chief entrance. I've saved the details for the next volume but he's a character that's challenging to draw in his own way.
- Tokiko's leg pillow was Kazuki's reward for working so hard. Woo-Hoo!

Hence... →

To be continued.

CHAPTER 15: DARK, HOT AND SWEET

...YOU'RE KOUSHAKU'S FATHER RIGHT?
KOUSHAKU WAS SUFFERING FROM AN ILLNESS.
TOK
THE SCHOOL AND POLICE HAVE BEEN CALLING ME ASKING QUESTIONS TOO. IT'S A NUISANCE.
TO TOP IT ALL OFF, HE'S BEEN MISSING SINCE THE "WIND GUST" INCIDENT AND THE POLICE CAME TO ASK QUESTIONS.
IF HE CAN'T ACCOMPLISH ANYTHING HE'S USELESS.
SO WHAT?
THAT JIRO WILL TAKE OVER AS THE HEAD OF THE CHOUNO ESTATE AND THAT HE IS NO LONGER NEEDED.
SLAMM
IF YOU SEE HIM TELL HIM..

CHAPTER 15:
DARK, HOT AND SWEET

YES? HELLO?
OH, BROTHER.
YEAH? TOKIKO?
武藤 2-B
ZOW
SHE'S FINE. I SWEAR ON NIGHTINGALE ...
I, NURSE MAHIRO WILL TAKE GOOD CARE OF HER!
...
DID SHE MAKE THAT OUTFIT?
MAYBE SHE HAS A UNIFORM FETISH?
IN THIS CASE, YOU'RE MORE LIKE A CARETAKER THAN A NURSE.
THIS ISN'T A PLACE KOUSHAKU WOULD GO.
PAPILLON ISN'T AT HIS HOUSE?
MAYBE HIS FATHER IS LYING?
YEAH, BUT FROM THE VIBE I GOT...
I WOULDN'T COME HOME EVEN IF I WERE KOUSHAKU.
DO YOU WANT A SHOT?
IRR!!
NO COMMENTS ALLOWED!

READ THIS WAY
NO... I'M SURE HE KNOWS WE WOULD THINK OF THOSE PLACES.
YEAH, HE'S PROBABLY AT THE HOSPITAL HE USED TO BE ADMITTED IN OR...
THE ABANDONED GHOST FACTORY.
I SEE... THEN OTHER PLACES HE MIGHT GO ARE...
HE CAN'T COUNT ON THE HOSPITAL OR FACTORY ANYMORE.
THE ONLY PLACE PAPILLON CAN COUNT ON NOW IS...
IT'S HUMAN PSYCHOLOGY TO FLEE SOMEWHERE FAMILIAR AND SAFE.
GOT IT! I'LL GO LOOK FOR HIM THERE!
DASH
AH! HEY, DON'T RUN!
YOU'LL COLLAPSE IF YOU PUSH YOURSELF TOO HARD.
I'M OKAY! FOR NOW!
FOR NOW?!

SLAM
ONLY ...
THREE AND A HALF HOURS LEFT...
TICK
TICK
RUMBLE
GROWL
...THAT'S RIGHT. I HAVEN'T EATEN SINCE YESTERDAY.
WHAT DO I WANT?
WHAT SHOULD I EAT FIRST WHEN I BECOME SUPER HUMAN?
BLUB
BLB

HUFF
HUFF
HUFF
HUFF
...I FOUND YOU KOUSHAKU.
HUFF
HUFF
HUFF
YOU'RE... KAZUKI.
THUMP
THUMP
THUMP
KOUSHA-KUUUUU!
VS SHH
KAZU-KIIIIIII!
GAACCK
SLAW
JOLT

TOKIKO'S SURPRISINGLY ENERGETIC.
WHAT DID I TELL YOU!
YOU GOT EXCITED AND FAINTED?
TWITCH
WHAT WAS THAT LOUD NOISE?
WHAT HAPPENED KAZUKI?
TWITCH
TWITCH
WAS THE ONLY PLACE HE COULD RUN TO!
THE STORAGE HOUSE WHERE HIS RESEARCH WAS KEPT...
I FOUND HIM, TOKIKO.
JUST AS YOU SUSPECTED, THE LAST THING HE COULD COUNT ON IS HIS GREAT-GREAT GRANDFATHER'S ALCHEMY RESEARCH.
WHEEZE
WHEEZE
WHEEZE
WHEEZE
ZUP
YEAH... HE WAS CONCERNED ABOUT YOU UNTIL THE END.
WASHIO MUST HAVE LOST IF YOU'RE STILL ALIVE.

IF HE CAN'T ACCOMPLISH ANYTHING HE'S USELESS.
SO WHAT?
HAND IT OVER.
THE ANTIDOTE AND HOMUNCULUS CORE...
I SWORE I WOULDN'T LET ANYONE ELSE DIE.
I CAN'T ALLOW YOU TO BECOME A HOMUN-CULUS.
FWIP
FWIP
YOU CAN HAVE THE ANTIDOTE.
BUT YOU CAN'T HAVE THIS.
SWUP
HURRY UP AND TAKE THE HOMUN-CULUS CORE.
NO WORDS CAN REACH HIM NOW.
IT'S USELESS TO TALK TO HIM.

YOU'RE GOING TO DIE ALONE AT THIS RATE.
KOUSHAKU, HUMAN OR HOMUNCULUS, EITHER WAY...
OKAY, TOKIKO.
BUT THERE'S ONE LAST THING I HAVE TO SAY...
NO ONE WILL REMEMBER YOU.
I DON'T CARE WHAT HAPPENS AFTER I DIE!
NO ONE WILL PRAY FOR YOU.
SO WHAT?
YOU'LL HAVE A GRAVE BUT NO ONE WILL BRING YOU FLOWERS OR BURN INCENSE FOR YOU.
WH...
S... O...
SO WHAT? YOU HYPOCRITE
IF YOU SWEAR TO MAKE IT UP TO THE PEOPLE WHO DIED ...
I'LL...

GR
AB
!!
GRAB
IT DOESN'T MATTER AFTER YOU'RE DEAD.
SO WHAT?
?!
A HYPOCRITE.
TOK
YOU'RE ...
WHAT DO YOU WANT, JIRO?
A KOUSHAKU CLONE?!
!

WHAT? YOU HAVEN'T TOLD HIM WHAT FATHER SAID?
I'M OFFICIALLY TAKING OVER THE OVER THE FAMILY ESTATE.
HIS YOUNGER BROTHER!
TOK
OH THAT?
I DON'T CARE ABOUT THAT ANYMORE.
OH... REALLY?
IT'S REALLY IMPORTANT TO ME.
ZWUF
I WAS BORN IN THE CHOUNO HOUSEHOLD BUT JUST BECAUSE I WAS BORN A YEAR LATER THAN YOU I'VE BEEN TREATED LIKE YOUR SPARE.
A NORMAL EDUCATION! A NORMAL SCHOOL! A NORMAL LIFE!
I DIDN'T EVEN GET A NAME WITH "SHAKU" IN IT, FROM OUR GREAT-GREAT GRANDFATHER'S NAME. I GOT A NORMAL NAME!
UNTIL YOU BECAME ILL...
I WAS A WORM CRAWLING ON THE GROUND!

I DIDN'T UNDERSTAND THE ENTIRE CONVERSATION BUT...
YOU'LL BE SAVED WITH THIS RIGHT?
BLUB
I CAN'T HAVE YOU RECOVER NOW.
TOK
THAT'S WHY...
THERE'S STILL SOME TIME LEFT UNTIL IT'S FINISHED!
YOU IDIOT! STOP!
KRAAA

HAAAAAA!
PAN!
HEEEEHHEHHEHHEH!
HURRY UP AND DIE!
DIE!
SEE?
NOBODY NEEDS YOU!
YOU'RE USELESS!
IDIOTS ...
YOU ...
GRIT
SHHHH
THIS FAMILY ...
IS CRAZY. ISN'T IT INTERESTING?

COME TO ME!!
GH
?!
TWITCH
YOU YEARN TO LIVE MORE THAN ANYONE!
YOU AND I ARE THE SAME!
WE'RE GONG TO BE REBORN AS A GRACEFUL PAPILLON!!
SO COME! NOW'S THE TIME WE BECOME A SUPER HUMAN ...
VS

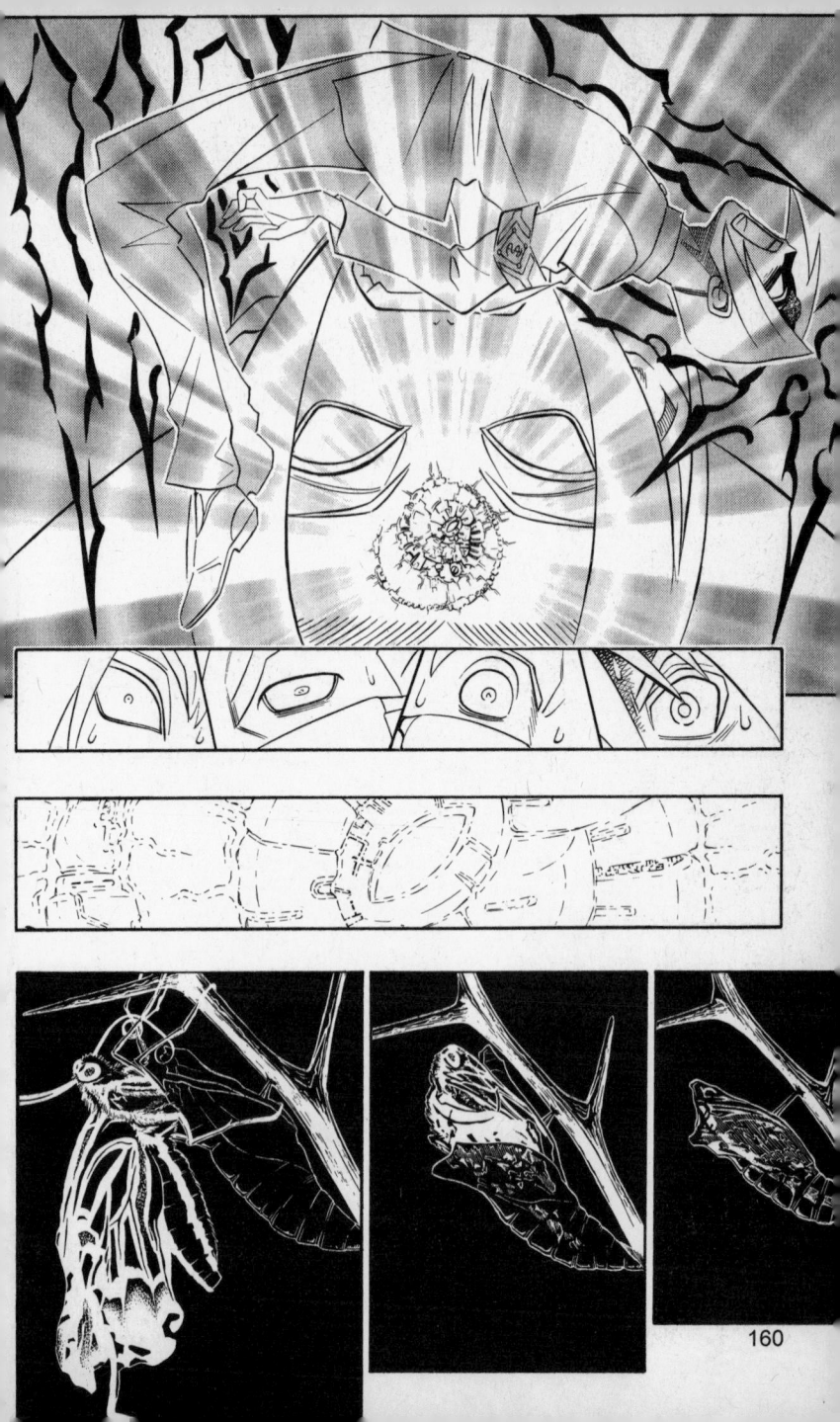

RAAB
?!?
YOU SAID... YOU WON'T ALLOW...
... KAZUKI.
ANYONE ELSE TO DIE?
W... WHAT THE ...?
WHAT JUST HAP-PENED?
FREEZE

TOO BAD.
GRAH?!
FSSSSW
URP
HMM ...
GULP

SO THIS IS THE FLAVOR OF HUMANS.
IT'S DARK AS THE DEVIL..
IT'S HOT AS HELL.
LICK
IT'S SWEET AS A KISS.
YUMM~YY
AAAA?
WHAT HAP-PENED?
WHAT'S GOING ON KAZUKI?
AAAH!
IT'LL BE CLOSE BUT...
I SWEAR I'LL BRING BACK THE ANTIDOTE!
I'M SORRY TOKIKO.
I HAVE TO FIGHT ONE MORE TIME.
WHAT?

Character File No.12

Koushaku Chouno

- Height: 180 cm; Weight: 64kg
- Born: June 26th; Cancer; Blood Type cisAB; 19 years old
- Favorites: Himself, butterflies, to make the impossible possible.
- Dislikes: Everything other than himself and butterflies. People who don't even try to make the impossible possible.
- Hobbies: Collecting insects, alchemy research
- Things he's good at: Coughing blood
- Affiliation: Private Ginsei Academy 3rd Year High School Student Class Room C (held back twice), Dorm resident

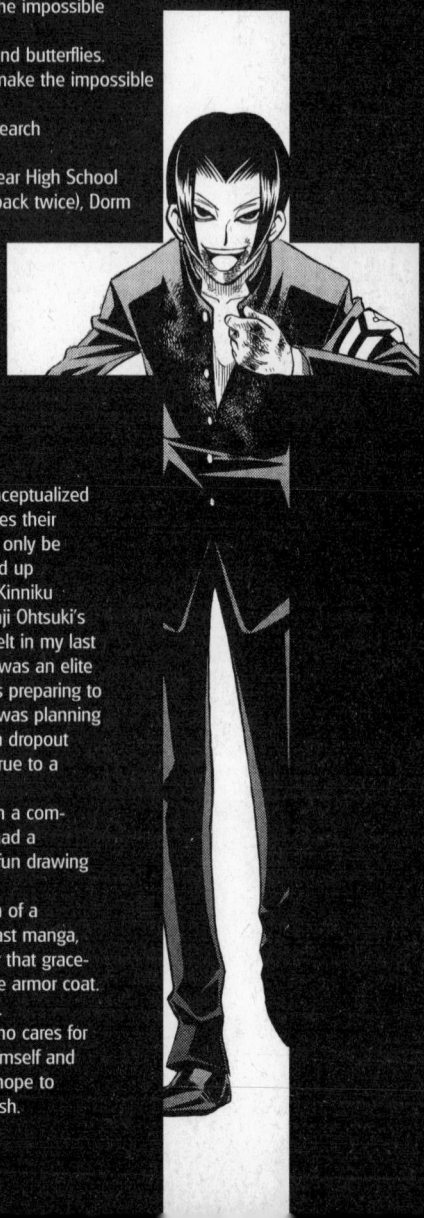

Author's Notes

- An outcast, every class has one. I conceptualized him from the type of person who hides their feeling and negative energy, and can only be described as magma and slime mixed up together. He was created combining Kinniku Shojotai song lyrics, characters in Kenji Ohtsuki's novels and the feeling of isolation I felt in my last year of high school. (My high school was an elite school and everyone in my class was preparing to take college entrance exams while I was planning to become a manga artist. I felt like a dropout more or less. Well, I guess that was true to a certain extent.)
- But somehow his character headed in a completely different direction. I've never had a character like this so it's sooo much fun drawing him.
- I got his design by altering the design of a character I didn't get to draw in my last manga, "Gun Blaze West." He was a matador that gracefully repelled bullets using his reactive armor coat. He was quite the ridiculous character.
- He is the polar opposite of Kazuki, who cares for others. Koushaku only cares about himself and continues to become more selfish. I hope to illustrate how he becomes more selfish.

CHAPTER 16:

BUTTERFLY OF BLACK DEATH

NOW I'M COMPLETE.
SWU
-PILLON!
PA-
KI
YOU SICKO!
CKK
BOOM
WE HIRE FROM THE YAKUZA, EH?
THE CHOUNO FAMILY BODYGUARDS ARE NICELY EQUIPPED.

BOOM
BOOM
BOOM
BOOM
BOOM
HAH.
HA-HAH.
IT HURTS BUT...
IT HURTS SO GOOD. ♡

DASH
HIEEE!
IT'S A MONSTER!
FWP
I'M NOT A MONSTER. I'M A SUPER HUMAN.
GYAAAAA!
VSHH

READ THIS WAY
... GUNSHOTS AND SCREAMS ...
KAZUKI ...
ZAH...
TAK
DID PAPILLON BECOME A HUMANOID HOMUNCULUS?
... I'M SORRY.
IT'S OKAY. IT'S NOT YOUR FAULT.
HURRY UP AND GET OUT OF THERE.
DRIP
YEAH, I KNOW ...
HE'S NO LONGER SOMETHING YOU CAN TAKE CARE OF YOURSELF.
JUST LIKE HUMANOID AND ANIMAL HOMUNCULUS ARE TWO DIFFERENT THINGS.
HUMANS AND MONKEYS ARE TWO DIFFERENT SPECIES.

BLISS
LICK
HAVE THE ANTIDOTE YET.
GRIT
BUT I DON'T...
RENKIN!
SHOOM
BUSO ...
DON'T KAZUKI!
THAT'S WHY ...

LXX
?!
SWWW
WON'T ACTIVATE?
WOOZE
I TOLD YOU...
THE BUSO RENKIN ...
YOU'RE ONLY ABLE TO MOVE RIGHT NOW BECAUSE OF THE HEALING EFFECTS OF THE TWO KAKUGANE.
YOU DON'T HAVE THE STRENGTH TO FIGHT!
CLENCH
SLAM

THAT SETTLES OUR MATCH.
HE CAN'T DESTROY A HOMUNCULUS WITHOUT THE BUSO RENKIN.
GROWL
I'M SURPRISED HOW MUCH ENERGY THIS BODY NEEDS.
I SHOULD EAT FIRST.
TICK
TICK
TICK
TUP
THREE MORE HOURS LEFT.
ALMOST MIDNIGHT... UNTIL THAT GIRL TURNS INTO A HOMUNCULUS THERE'S ONLY ...
CREAK
SLAM
YOU STAY HERE AND ...
DESPAIR AT YOUR WEAKNESS.

READ THIS WAY
TUP
!
TOK
JIRO?
WHAT'S WITH THE OUTFIT?
TOK
SHHHHHF
HMF. WELL, WE LOOK IDENTICAL SO...
JIRO, EH...

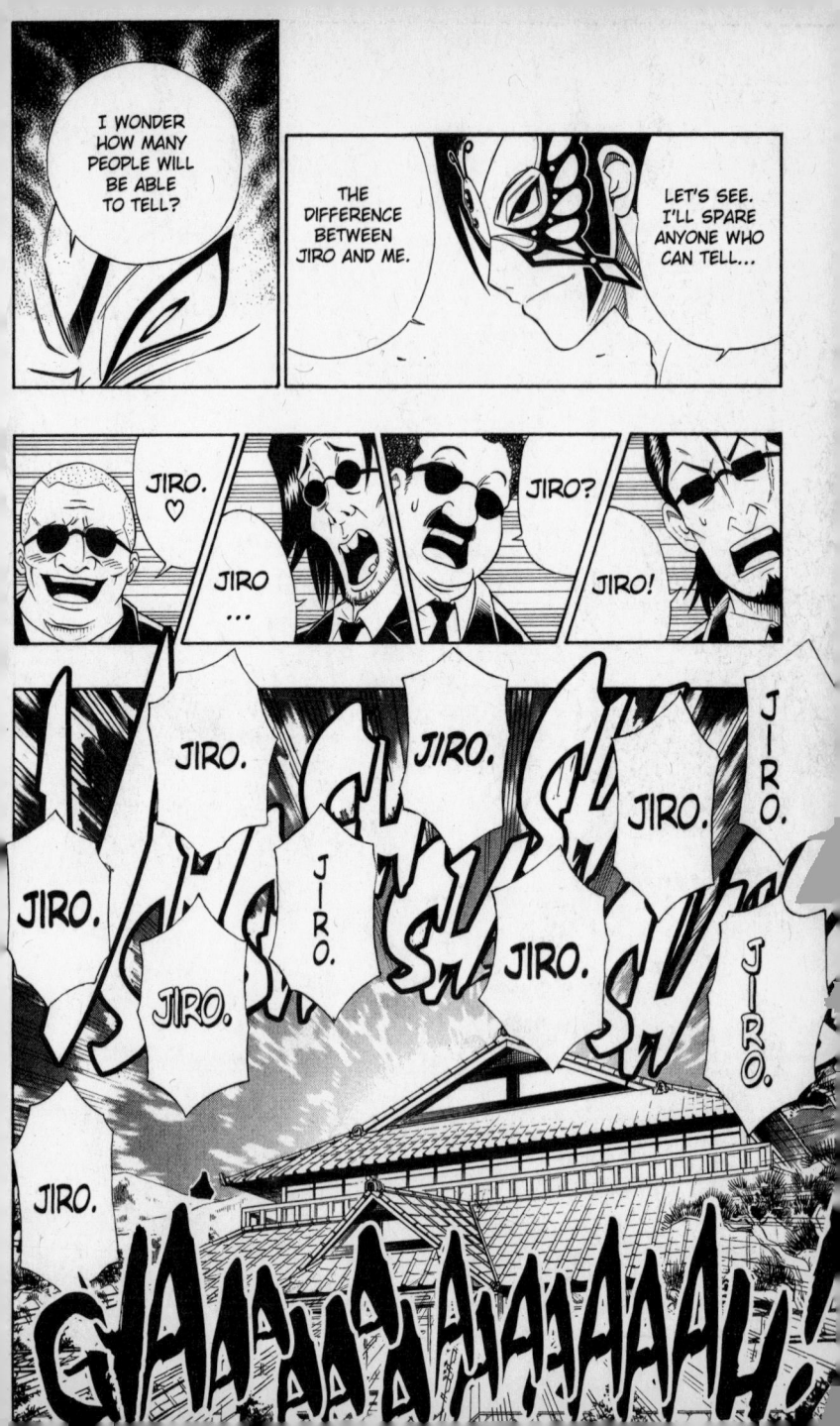
I WONDER HOW MANY PEOPLE WILL BE ABLE TO TELL?
THE DIFFERENCE BETWEEN JIRO AND ME.
LET'S SEE. I'LL SPARE ANYONE WHO CAN TELL...
JIRO. ♡
JIRO ...
JIRO?
JIRO!
JIRO.
JIRO.
JIRO.
JIRO.
JIRO.
JIRO.
JIRO.
JIRO.
JIRO.
JIRO.
GAAAAAAAAAAAAAAAH!

TURNED INTO A MONSTER !!
JIRO ...
ARE THEY PLAYING AROUND?
IT'S NOISY!
GYAAAAA...
DAD.

WHAT KIND OF PARTY ARE WE HAVING TONIGHT?
OH! WHAT A SPLENDID OUTFIT, JIRO!
VSSH
SSH
VSSH
GYAAA
A
RO...
JI...
IT'S A MEMORIAL TRIBUTE TO THE PASSING OF KOUSHAKU CHOUNO.
WELL, LET'S SEE ...

I GET IT...
FSSW
HE DIED A LONG TIME AGO ...
KOUSHAKU CHOUNO DIDN'T DIE TONIGHT...
IT'S ANOTHER KIND OF PARTY.
THEN FROM HERE ON...
OF SUPER HUMAN PAPILLON!
A CELEBRATION OF THE BIRTH...

GET OUT OF THERE NOW KAZUKI!
HELLO, TOKIKO ...
... ZUKI ...
... KI ...
SU

LEAVE PAPILLON TO THE WARRIOR WHO TAKES MY POST.
IT'S OKAY. I'VE ALREADY ACCEPTED MY FATE!
I HAVE TO DEFEAT KOUSHAKU ...
I CAN'T! I DON'T HAVE THE ANTIDOTE...

YOU DON'T HAVE ANY STRENGTH LEFT. YOU'VE DONE WELL.
HURRY UP AND COME HOME.
BUT ...
COME BACK HOME!
ROLL

CAN YOU PASS ME TO MAHIRO AND EVERYONE?
THE PHONE ...

READ THIS WAY
KAZUKI! DO YOU NEED HELP?
YEAH! I'LL SHOW THEM THE TRUE POWERS OF MY GREASED HAIR!
KAH
AH, KAZUKI? I HID THE DIRTY GIRL'S MAGAZINE THAT WAS UNDER YOUR PILLOW.
YOU NEED TO BE MORE CAREFUL. TOKIKO WILL PROBABLY BE FINE BUT IF MAHIRO SEES IT SHE'LL KILL YOU.
PSST PSST
KAZUKI, MAKE SURE YOU COME IN THROUGH THE BACK DOOR.
Hey, I'm Kazuki.
THE CLASS LEADERS HAVE THEIR EYES ON YOU LATELY SO DON'T SCREW UP, OKAY?
HI BROTHER.
DON'T WORRY ABOUT TOKIKO. LEAVE IT TO ME!
YEAH, I WAS JUST PEELING HER AN APPLE.

HERE, CARRY ON WITH YOUR STRAW-BERRY TALKS.
...
THERE WON'T BE ANY LEFT IF YOU DON'T COME HOME SOON.
KAZUKI.
I'LL GET THE ANTIDOTE ...
AND PROMISE TO COME HOME!
WAKE
I'M STARTING TO FEEL A LITTLE BETTER!
CRASH
HUH?
I'M GOING TO BORROW ...
YOUR POWERS.
THAT'S WHY ...

A CELEBRATION OF THE BIRTH OF SUPER HUMAN PAPILLON!
IT'S A LITTLE EARLY BUT...
DID YOU MOPE IN DESPAIR?
CRACK
I'LL CREATE A SUPER LARGE BEACON...
FIT FOR SUCH A COLD NIGHT'S SKY.
THERE'S SOMETHING I HAVE TO DO.
BOOM
I'LL TURN EVERY-THING INTO ASHES!
THIS WORLD HAD NO NEED FOR KOUSHAKU CHOUNO.
WHAT?
ZWA
KOU-SHAKU!
VS SH

?!
MY KAKU-GANE?
I'M GOING TO BORROW YOUR POWERS.
DOUBLE...
BU-SO REN-KIN!!
FLASH
XLIV
XLIV
LXX

LET'S FINISH THIS KOUSHAKU ...
THIS WILL BE MY FINAL ATTACK!!

- Koushaku's father. He only sees worth in geniuses and likes to categorize people as either necessary or unnecessary. His love for his sons runs deep but his convictions run deeper.
- He's separated with his wife and is currently in the middle of a divorce.

Author's Notes

- To illustrate where Koushaku got his twisted personality I introduced his family. "A son strives to surpass his father," so I decided he kills his father.
- Koushaku's weird fashion taste runs in the family.

Shishaku Chouno

Character File No.13

The People of the Chouno Family

- Koushaku's younger brother. He is talented and gifted but as the second son he is named Jiro. His brother is his biggest enemy.

Author's Notes

- To emphasize that Jiro does not get acknowledged by anyone, I made him look exactly the same as Koushaku. It also symbolizes Jiro as the mirror image of Koushaku. I had a lot of fun drawing his twisted smile.
- It wasn't his fault. I felt sorry for him. (Praying)

Jiro Chouno

- A Yakuza group on good terms with the Chouno family sent them as bodyguards. They oversee the security of the estate and "fix" any kind of problems that may arise.
- They are pretty strong.
- One of them is gay.

Author's Notes

- If humans were going to get eaten I thought I'd go all out instead of making it seem gruesome so I needed a lot of people. I treated them as throwaway soldiers.
- I thought drawing guys in black suits and sunglasses might be lame but once I started drawing, I realized they were easy to draw and surprisingly I was able to give them a lot of character.
- They are "Men in Black."

MY FINAL ATTACK!!
THIS WILL BE ...
LET'S FINISH THIS KOU-SHAKU.
CHAPTER 17:
FADE TO BLACK
INTER-ESTING... BUT!
THE DOUBLE LANCE ...
BZ
BZ
BZ
BZ
BZ
BZ
伸宏
和月

DRIP
TUP
HUFF
HUFF
TUP
EVEN THE DOUBLE LANCES ARE UNSTABLE...
THEY CAN DISASSEMBLE ANY MINUTE.
TUP
TUP
TUP
TUP
YOU'RE COVERED IN WOUNDS ...
AND COMPLETELY EXHAUSTED.
HUFF
HUFF
YOU THINK YOU CAN WIN LIKE THAT? YOU MAKE ME WANT TO SPEW OUT LAUGHING!
HE'S LOSING ALL HIS STRENGTH! IF THE SITUATION IS PROLONGED HE'LL DIE BEFORE HE EVEN FIGHTS!
KAZUKI!

GLCH
GLLCH
BLCHH
TP
I SEE... LISTEN KAZUKI.
PAPILLON!
TP
WOOZE
AK ...
TP
I DON'T SEE IT ANYWHERE ...
KAZUKI... DOES PAPILLON HAVE AN EMBLEM?
TP
HA ...
THAT REPULSIVE SOUND...
TP
KOUSHAKU IS SPEWING BLOOD.
TP
YOU USED AN UNFINISHED HOMUNCULUS CORE SO THERE ARE FLAWS!
YOUR TRANSFOR-MATION WAS A FAILURE!

WITH YOUR "IMMORTAL, SICKLY BODY"...
YOU WILL SUFFER IN "PAIN AND AGONY FOR ETERNITY."
YOU BECAME A SUPER HUMAN...
WITH YOUR SICKLY BODY.
THERE'S ANOTHER NEW LIFE!
RIGHT IN FRONT OF ME!
TUP
TUP
THAT...
IS THE RESULT OF YOU WANTING TO LIVE WHILE SACRIFICING COUNTLESS PEOPLE.
YOU DESERVE IT.
THERE ARE OTHER METHODS.
BUT...
GRIN
I MESSED UP...

READ THIS WAY
IF YOU TRY OPENING IT WITH ANYTHING BUT THIS KEY IT WILL EXPLODE.
THE ANTIDOTE IS IN THE BOX BEHIND THE INCUBATOR.
SWIF
TUP
TP
TUP
TP
TP
KAZUKI!
AFTER I EAT YOU AND TAKE THE KAKUGANE, THE GIRL WILL TURN INTO A HOMUNCULUS AND BECOME MY SUBJECT.
COME AND GET IT!
LICK
I WON'T LET THAT HAPPEN!
TUP
THEN I'LL TURN THIS WORLD INTO ASHES!
TP
I'LL STOP YOU!
TP
TUP

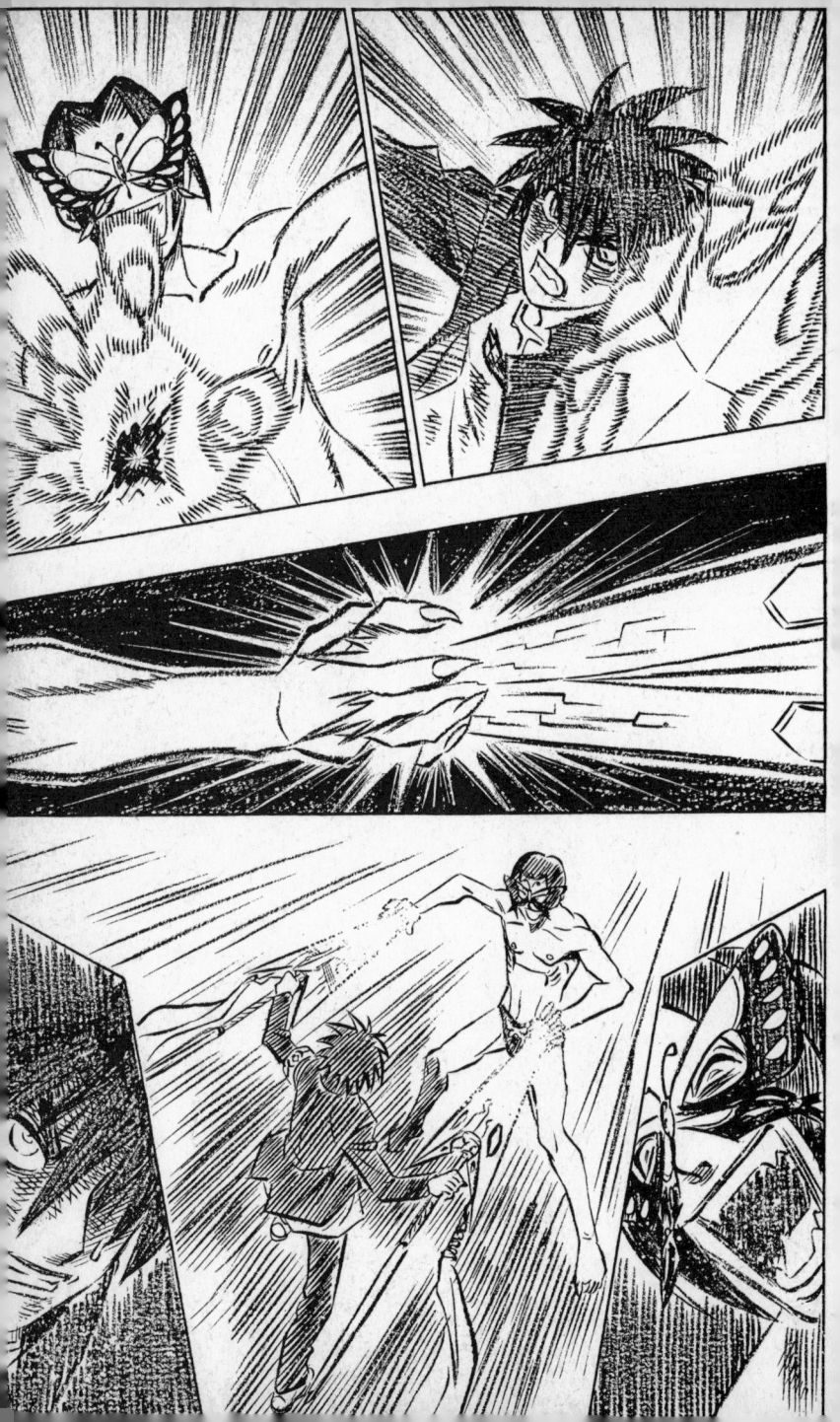

WOOM
HUFF
HUFF
HFF
HFF
THIS CAN'T BE...
I MAY NOT BE COMPLETE, BUT I'M SUPER HUMAN.
HOW COULD A HUMAN DEFEAT ME...

THIS BUSO RENKIN...
?
THAT'S WHY...
I WAS A LITTLE STRONGER THAN YOU BECAUSE YOU NEVER FOUGHT BEFORE.
...IS OWERFUL!
EVERYTHING YOU KNOW!
I'M AN ORDINARY HUMAN BUT...
I'VE COME THIS FAR AFTER BEING IN MULTIPLE LIFE OR DEATH BATTLES.
PLUS THE KEY TO THE ANTIDOTE IS IN MY STOMACH. ARE YOU GOING TO WAIT UNTIL I DIGEST IT OUT?
COME ON. WHAT ARE YOU GOING TO DO?
...HMF. YOU'RE STRONGER AND YOU DEFEATED ME. SO WHAT ARE YOU GOING TO DO NOW?
I CAN'T GO BACK TO BEING A HUMAN SO I HAVE TO KEEP EATING PEOPLE.
AAA... MY NAME ...
I'M SORRY.
KOUSHAKU CHOUNO.

YOU HYPO-CRITE.
DON'T APOLOGIZE.
TNK
SHHH

HUFF
HUFF
SWIP
HUFF ...
KAZU ...
KAZUKI!?
CLANK
BEEP
BEEP
BEEP
THU
TOKI... KO....
SMASH
...
THE ANTIDOTE TO TOKIKO ...
SOMEONE ... ANYONE ...
AT LEAST TOKIKO ...
I COULDN'T KEEP MY WORD BUT...
"I WON'T ALLOW ANYONE ELSE TO DIE."

BRAVO!
WELL DONE, KAZUKI MUTO.
WE'LL BE BACK AFTER MIDNIGHT WHEN THEY FINISH PATROLLING THE BUILDING.
THEY'VE TOUGHENED UP THE DORM RULES BECAUSE OF THE VARIOUS INCIDENTS LATELY.
TICK
TICK
WE'RE GOING TO BACK TO OUR ROOMS NOW.

SURE ...
I'M FINE. SORRY TO WORRY YOU.
YOU LOOK REALLY EXHAUSTED.
ARE YOU SURE YOU'LL BE ALL RIGHT ALONE?
CLICK
OKAY.
SEE YOU IN A LITTLE BIT.
OR ELSE I'LL HURT THEM...
I HAVE TO HURRY ...
KAZUKI ...
AT LEAST I HOPE YOU ARE OKAY...

CHIEF!
WAR-RIOR ...
WARRIOR TOKIKO.
IT'S NOT LIKE YOU.
PLOP
HERE'S THE ANTIDOTE.
I MOVED KAZUKI MUTO TO A SAFE PLACE.
WE'LL TALK LATER. HURRY UP AND GO GET HIM.

...
IT'S LIGHT.
THE SUN IS RISING.
IT'S MORNING ...
!!!
AA.
AA ...

YOUR BUSO RENKIN'S ENERGY...
UP CLOSE, IT'S A GOLDEN YELLOW COLOR SIMILAR TO THE RAYS OF THE SUN.
IT TOOK ME A WHILE TO NAME YOUR LANCE BUT WHAT DO YOU THINK OF...
"SUNLIGHT HEART."
DO YOU LIKE IT?
KAZUKI.
DID YOU KNOW?

VOLUME 2: FADE TO BLACK (THE END)

Coming Next Volume

An old enemy with a slight butterfly fetish once thought to be destroyed makes a surprising comeback! Impressed with Kazuki's progress in such a short time, Captain Bravo recruits him as a full-fledged Alchemist Warrior! And he orders Tokiko to enlist in the same school as Kazuki! All this, plus the appearance of a new Homuculus that has the power to use a Buso Renkin!

Available in December 2006!

12 RINGS TO RAISE THE DEAD...
ONE MAN TO FIND THEM

$7.99

ZOMBIEPOWDER
SHONEN JUMP MANGA
Story & Art by
Tite Kubo
volume 1

ZOMBIEPOWDER
1
Tite Kubo

ZOMBIE POWDER VOL. 1
ON SALE NOW!

New Series!

ZOMBIEPOWDER

viz media

SJ

RATED T FOR OLDER TEEN

ON SALE AT:
www.shonenjump.com
Also available at your local bookstore and comic store.

SHONEN JUMP

ZOMBIE POWDER © 1999 by Tite Kubo/SHUEISHA Inc.

Tell us what you think about SHONEN JUMP manga!

Our survey is now available online.
Go to: ***www.SHONENJUMP.com/mangasurvey***

Help us make our product offering better!

BLEACH © 2001 by Tite Kubo/SHUEISHA Inc. NARUTO © 1999 by Masashi Kishimoto/SHUEISHA Inc.
DEATH NOTE © 2003 by Tsugumi Ohba, Takeshi Obata/SHUEISHA Inc. ONE PIECE © 1997 by Eiichiro Oda/SHUEISHA Inc.

LAKE VILLA DISTRICT LIBRARY
1001 EAST GRAND AVENUE
LAKE VILLA, IL 60046
(847) 356-7711

SUBSCRIBE TODAY & BECOME A MEMBER OF THE SHONEN JUMP SUBSCRIBER-CLUB...

You'll get:

*Access to Exclusive Online Content!

*50% Savings Off the Newsstand Price!

*Exclusive Premiums!

All this available ONLY to Subscribers!

SHONEN JUMP

THE WORLD'S MOST POPULAR MANGA™

FILL OUT THE SUBSCRIPTION CARD ON THE OTHER SIDE, OR SUBSCRIBE ONLINE AT:

www.shonenjump.com

Save 50% off the newsstand price!

SHONEN JUMP™

THE WORLD'S MOST POPULAR MANGA

SUBSCRIBE TODAY and SAVE 50% OFF the cover price PLUS enjoy all the benefits of the SHONEN JUMP SUBSCRIBER CLUB, exclusive online content & special gifts ONLY AVAILABLE to SUBSCRIBERS!

☑ **YES!** Please enter my 1 year subscription (12 issues) to *SHONEN JUMP* at the INCREDIBLY LOW SUBSCRIPTION RATE of $29.95 and sign me up for the SHONEN JUMP Subscriber Club!

Only $29.95!

NAME

ADDRESS

CITY STATE ZIP

E-MAIL ADDRESS

☐ MY CHECK IS ENCLOSED ☐ BILL ME LATER

CREDIT CARD: ☐ VISA ☐ MASTERCARD

ACCOUNT # EXP. DATE

SIGNATURE

CLIP AND MAIL TO

SHONEN JUMP
Subscriptions Service Dept.
P.O. Box 515
Mount Morris, IL 61054-0515

Make checks payable to: **SHONEN JUMP.**
Canada add US $12. No foreign orders. Allow 6-8 weeks for delivery.

P6SJGN YU-GI-OH! © 1996 by Kazuki Takahashi / SHUEISHA Inc.

LAKE VILLA DISTRICT LIBRARY
3 1981 00362 4784